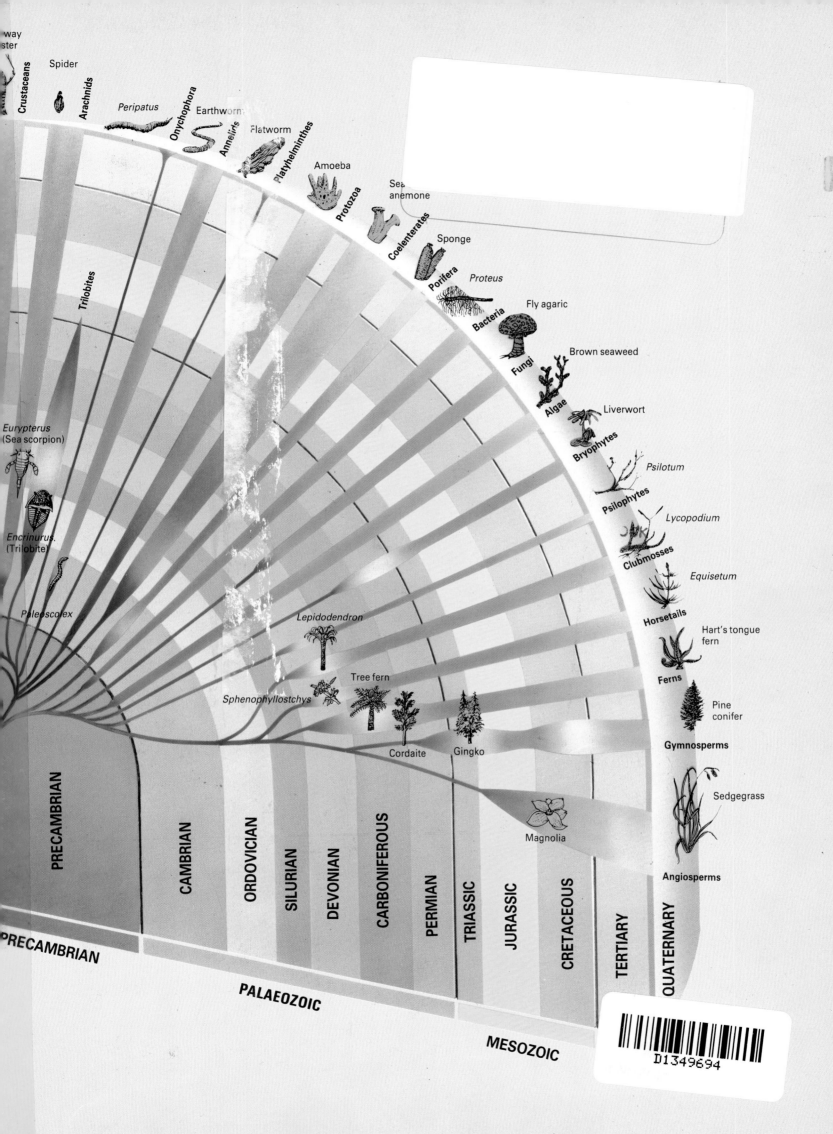

Crustaceans

Spider

Arachnids

Peripatus

Onychophora Earthworm

Annelids Flatworm

Platyhelminthes

Amoeba

Protozoa

Sea anemone

Coelenterates Sponge

Porifera *Proteus*

Bacteria Fly agaric

Fungi Brown seaweed

Algae Liverwort

Bryophytes *Psilotum*

Psilophytes *Lycopodium*

Clubmosses *Equisetum*

Horsetails Hart's tongue fern

Ferns Pine conifer

Gymnosperms

Sedgegrass

Angiosperms

Trilobites

Eurypterus (Sea scorpion)

Encrinurus. (Trilobite)

Paleoscolex

Lepidodendron

Tree fern

Sphenophyllostchys

Cordaite Gingko

Magnolia

PRECAMBRIAN

PRECAMBRIAN

CAMBRIAN

ORDOVICIAN

SILURIAN

DEVONIAN

CARBONIFEROUS

PERMIAN

TRIASSIC

JURASSIC

CRETACEOUS

TERTIARY

QUATERNARY

PALAEOZOIC

MESOZOIC

The Story of Evolution

Ron Taylor

WARD LOCK LIMITED

Editorial

Author
Ron Taylor

Editorial Consultant
Dr Jeremy Cherfas

Editor
Angela Wilkinson

Assistant Editor
Jane Collin

Dictionary compiled by
Ron Taylor

Editor's note. On pages 72 to 75 of this book you will find a dictionary of evolution. Many of the terms used throughout the main chapters are printed in SMALL CAPITALS. You will find an entry in the dictionary which will give you a further explanation of these terms.

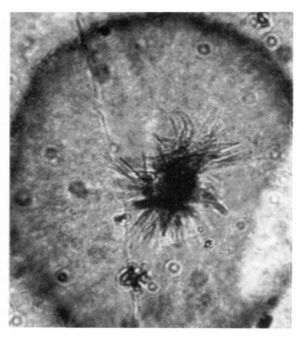

First published in Great Britain 1980 by Ward Lock Ltd, 116 Baker Street, London, W1M 2BB, a Pentos Company.

© **Grisewood and Dempsey Limited 1980**

Designed and produced by Grisewood and Dempsey Ltd, Grosvenor House, 141–143 Drury Lane, London WC2

Printed in Italy by Vallardi Industrie Grafiche, Milan.

British Library Cataloguing in Publication Data
Taylor, Ron
    The Story of Evolution
    1. Evolution – Juvenile Literature
    i. Title
    575   QH367.1

ISBN 0 7063 5926 7

Contents

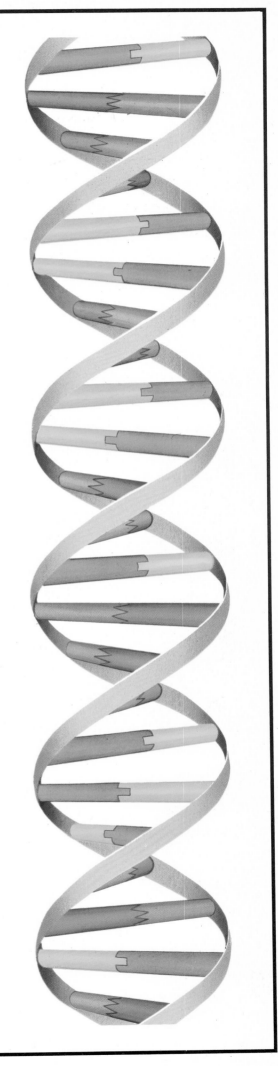

Chapter *1*
The Idea of
Evolution

Charles Darwin's books, *On the Origin of Species* and *The Descent of Man*, created a tremendous fuss in Victorian England. In particular, the idea that man could have descended from ape-like creatures was abhorrent to many people. That the church was violently opposed to it was understandable. For most of Christianity's long history, any important idea that conflicted with church doctrine was taboo – and the idea of biological evolution contradicted Genesis. But Darwin himself had not invented the idea of evolution. A generation before him, scientists of the Age of Enlightenment, such as Jean Baptiste de Lamarck and Count BUFFON, had spoken out boldly for the idea. Their explanations for evolution, however, were at best rather vague. Darwin's own explanation was anything but vague, and this is what gave it such force. Crammed with facts gained from accurate observations made over many years, *The Origin of Species* was difficult to refute. Evolution had come to stay.

Yet Darwin died knowing his theory was incomplete. It explained how populations change and evolve, but it failed to show convincingly how individual parents hand on their characteristics to their offspring. An obscure monk, Gregor Mendel, had already discovered the laws of heredity in Darwin's lifetime, but his work was not given the attention it deserved until the early years of our own century.

Charles Darwin's ideas on evolution began to form during his long visit to South America and the Galápagos Islands. The iguanas of those islands show clear indications of evolutionary change. The partly webbed feet of this marine iguana are possessed by no other iguana, and are adaptations which help fit it to its special way of life.

Darwin's Discoveries

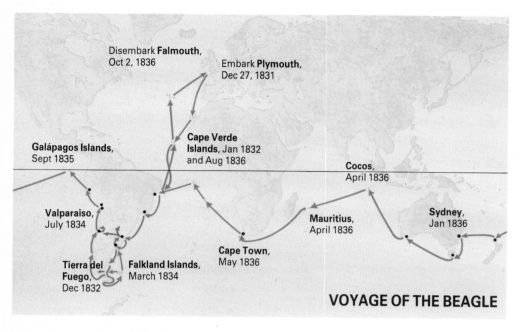

Disembark **Falmouth**,
Oct 2, 1836

Embark **Plymouth**,
Dec 27, 1831

Cape Verde Islands, Jan 1832 and Aug 1836

Galápagos Islands,
Sept 1835

Cocos,
April 1836

Valparaiso,
July 1834

Mauritius,
April 1836

Sydney,
Jan 1836

Tierra del Fuego,
Dec 1832

Falkland Islands,
March 1834

Cape Town,
May 1836

VOYAGE OF THE BEAGLE

Above: The young Charles Darwin's voyage of discovery as naturalist on HMS *Beagle*, 1831–1836.

Left: Charles Darwin in his later years.

Below: Conrad Marten's watercolour of HMS *Beagle* in the waters of Murray Narrow, Tierra del Fuego, the chilly southernmost tip of the American continent. In South America, Darwin discovered strong evidence of geological and biological evolution.

When, in 1831, the young Charles DARWIN set out on his famous voyage in HMS *Beagle*, he was already an experienced naturalist and collector of insects. He held no strong evolutionary opinions, but he read with great interest the works of LAMARCK, which maintained that FOSSILS are evidence for the evolution of living creatures, and of Charles Lyell, who argued powerfully the case for the slow evolution of the Earth's rocks.

The exciting ideas of these two authorities directly contradicted the Bible's account of special creation, which says that the Earth and all its inhabitants were made in six days. (The date then usually proposed was 4004 BC.) But Baron CUVIER, greatest of the older living scientific naturalists at the time, persisted in believing in a form of special creation. Darwin read and admired him, too.

In the five years of his voyage, Darwin made the discoveries that turned him into a true evolutionist. These demonstrated not only that living creatures change with time – fossils had already shown this to many scientists. Darwin's acute observations, backed up by his strong imagination, also revealed to him just *how* creatures change.

Always the most careful and painstaking of scientists, Darwin did not publish his new explanation of the evolutionary process for more than twenty years after the end of his voyage. Much of this time he spent sifting the many valuable specimens he had brought back, and in collecting yet further evidence from specimens sent him by other scientific travellers. Indeed, his first publications were as much about geography and geology as about biology.

Corals, Sloths and Varieties

In South America, Darwin had found bones of such remarkable and ponderous animals as the giant sloth, a creature then only recently extinct, that had towered six metres (19 ft) high as it browsed off treetops. These highlights of his early discoveries had, however, less profound results for evolutionary theory than his growing awareness, formed from many observations, of VARIATION.

In South America he noticed how animal SPECIES often varied on either side of a natural barrier such as a mountain chain. When he reached the Galápagos Islands, he found still more extraordinary animal populations, containing very significant variation in species between one island and another.

The Galápagos, on the Equator 1000 km (621 miles) off the north-western coast of South America, have probably never been connected geologically with that continent. Their dominant large animals are not MAMMALS, as in most other parts of the world, but REPTILES such as giant tortoises and iguanas.

Darwin observed how the shells of Galápagos tortoises vary, on one island being high-domed, on the next more flattened in shape. Perhaps he wondered what purpose the Creator could have had in allocating the tortoises of each island such special shapes.

The smaller dominant animals of the Galápagos are birds, among which is an extraordinary flightless cormorant. But Darwin's interest was captured most strongly by the islands' finches. He saw that the beaks of these birds range all the way from slim insect-pickers to powerful nutcrackers. Yet in most other respects, the finches were obviously the 'same sort' of bird. What could this signify?

Above: From the South American mainland, Darwin voyaged to the Galápagos Islands, where, among other fascinating evolutionary leftovers, he found these giant tortoises. Reptiles are the dominant large land animals of the Galápagos, not mammals as in most other parts of the world.

Left: One of the most remarkable fossil animals discovered in South America is *Megatherium*, the giant ground sloth. It stood six metres (19 ft) high, weighed more than an elephant, and was probably brought to extinction by man.

11

Natural Selection

1　　　　2　　　　3　　　　4

Darwin's finches, as they have come to be called, are the most famous historical example of what biologists now know as ADAPTIVE RADIATION. Darwin found fourteen varieties of finch on the Galápagos, each with a beak of distinct and appropriate 'design'. These finches looked to Darwin as though they had descended from one, or at most a few, types of finch that had landed on the islands at some unknown time in the past.

The question remained, how could such changes occur? The first point to be considered in answering this question is that the changes would have occurred in a *population* of finches. In every population that Darwin had looked at, he had observed variation. Among Galápagos tortoises, the sizes and shapes of the shells varied considerably, depending on which island the tortoises came from. In any original population of finches, the sizes and shapes of the finches' beaks would also have varied to some extent, even if at that time all the finches had fed in the same way.

On the islands, food of many kinds was available. Perhaps some of the original finches, those with the narrowest beaks, did best when they concentrated on insect food,

Above: Examples of Galápagos finches sketched by Darwin. These four closely related species have evolved contrasting beaks, of which (1) is a stout nutcracker; (2) is averagely finch-like, and (3) and (4) are slimmer insect-pickers.

Below: Natural selection usually works too slowly for any one person to be able to witness evolution in action. However, British populations of the dark, or melanic, variety of the peppered moth appeared in only 50 years or so. This happened because of the Industrial Revolution, which blackened trees in many parts of Britain. Melanic moths resting on these trees were less easily seen and picked off by birds, and so their populations grew.

while those with the broadest beaks had selected more seeds and nuts for their diet.

Darwin and Malthus

At this point in his thoughts about evolution, Darwin read the *Essay on Population* by the economist Thomas MALTHUS, which describes a struggle for existence in which human population numbers always rise when more than enough food and other necessities are available, and always fall, by starvation, disease, crime and war, when these necessities run short.

Darwin saw that here was a force, or mechanism, to explain such population changes as those of the Galápagos finches. As the original finches increased in numbers, there would come a time when food on the islands would run short. So, in the struggle for existence, those birds with beaks best fitted for each type of available food would tend to survive in the greatest numbers, and those with beaks less well fitted would decline.

If beak shape could be inherited, the birds selected by nature to survive would pass on their beak shapes, together with their other characteristics, to their offspring, so that in time new populations of finches would arise, having beaks much more specialized for particular kinds of food.

Darwin and Wallace

As Darwin laboured over his massive evidence for *On The Origin of Species*, a younger English naturalist, Alfred Russell WALLACE, working quite independently in the jungles of Indonesia, also read Malthus and also arrived at the idea of evolution by the SURVIVAL OF THE FITTEST. Moreover, Wallace's studies of variation among and between animal populations, while by no means as extensive as Darwin's, nevertheless were of great importance. Wallace's line is still used to separate the very different mammal populations of the Bali and Borneo sides of Indonesia.

In 1857, Wallace sent Darwin his essay *On the Law which has Regulated the Introduction of New Species* and this at last forced Darwin to publish his great work. 'The Law', in both Darwin's and Wallace's terminology, is NATURAL SELECTION.

Fossils and Theories

Fossils were the first strong evidence for biological evolution, and they remain today its most undisputed record. However, they are a very incomplete record because most animals and plants of the past died without leaving fossils. Also, in Darwin's day, the majority of fossils still remained concealed in rocks, not then discovered.

But even before Darwin, scientists had looked at fossils as evidence of a past progress of life. Baron Cuvier saw in them evidence of repeated creations and annihilations, an understandable idea in view of the great gaps that exist in the fossil record.

Lamarck, on the other hand, regarded fossils as evidence of evolution. He was right and Cuvier wrong, yet the fossil record certainly provided little evidence for Lamarck's own theory of evolution.

This said that evolution proceeds from the inheritance of ACQUIRED CHARACTERISTICS. That is, characteristics 'striven for' by an individual during its lifetime are handed on to its offspring, and so accumulate to produce evolutionary change. The rather comical example most often quoted is that of the giraffe's long neck. Lamarck's theory says that the neck was acquired by ancestral giraffes, all of which were striving to reach leaves on higher branches. Darwin's theory says that the giraffe has a long neck because, in a population of giraffes, some of which have longer and some shorter necks, natural selection favours individuals with the longer necks.

Proof and Evidence

Evidence is lacking to show that acquired characteristics play any decisive role in evolutionary change. But then neither Darwin's nor Wallace's theory can be proved by

Right: The Grand Canyon of Arizona, USA, about two kilometres or more than a mile deep, exposes rocks which bear fossils ranging in size and age from primitive single-cell algae to dinosaurs and large trees.

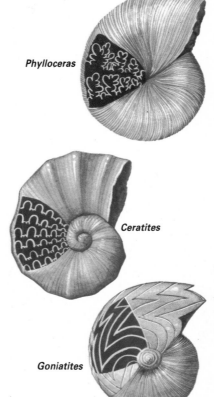

Phylloceras

Ceratites

Goniatites

Above: Among the best-preserved and most elegant of fossils are the ammonites. These extinct relatives of today's nautilus, octopuses and squids have a wide range of patterns and forms, and a long geological record. This makes them very useful to geologists for dating and characterizing rocks.

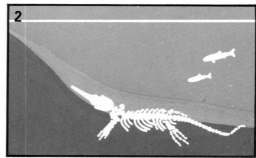

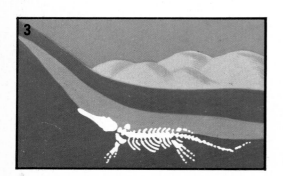

HOW FOSSILS ARE FORMED
Stages in the formation of a large fossil, that of the marine reptile called an ichthyosaur.
(1) The animal dies and its body sinks to the sea bed.
(2) Its skeleton is exposed as its flesh decays.
(3) The bone of its skeleton is gradually petrified, or replaced by harder mineral substances. At the same time, the fossil is covered with sediments which harden into rock, and earth movements raise the fossil-bearing rock above water.
(4) This exposes the rock to weathering or erosion, which eventually uncovers the fossil.

Right: Each bone of this extinct ichthyosaur is exactly represented in its fossil, first laid down in the rocks of Street, Somerset, about 150 million years ago.

direct observation. Even the much fuller fossil record that we have today will not show conclusively that natural selection is the method by which populations of living organisms evolve.

What the fossil record does show is that during the 3500 million years that life has existed on Earth, simpler organisms came first and more complex organisms followed later, undoubtedly arising from the simpler ones. It also shows that simple, plant-like organisms preceded, and gave rise to, simple animal-like organisms – both of which have left their tiny fossils in the rocks.

Sometimes, but not often, fossils occur of large populations of organisms which are fundamentally similar but which show a wide range of variations of form, of about the same order as the variations in the Galápagos finches' beaks. Such are the AMMONITES, common fossils of sea creatures with spirally coiled shells, related to the squids and nautilus still living today.

Small variations in ammonite shells and other parts are of the 'right size' for natural selection. By providing small advantages in certain situations or ENVIRONMENTS, some of these variations would have contributed to the evolutionary success of some ammonites, leading to their persistence in the rocks. Of course, other variations would act in the opposite way, causing some ammonites to become extinct earlier than others.

But to prove his theory of evolution conclusively, Darwin would have needed to know what causes variation in populations, and also in what ways these various characteristics are handed down from parents to offspring. He was very well aware that he did not have good answers to these questions, and he strongly suspected that no one else of his time could answer them either. The answers have come only gradually since his day, and are later, fascinating chapters in the story of evolution.

Above: Fossil leaves of plants that lived about 15 million years ago, in the Miocene Epoch.

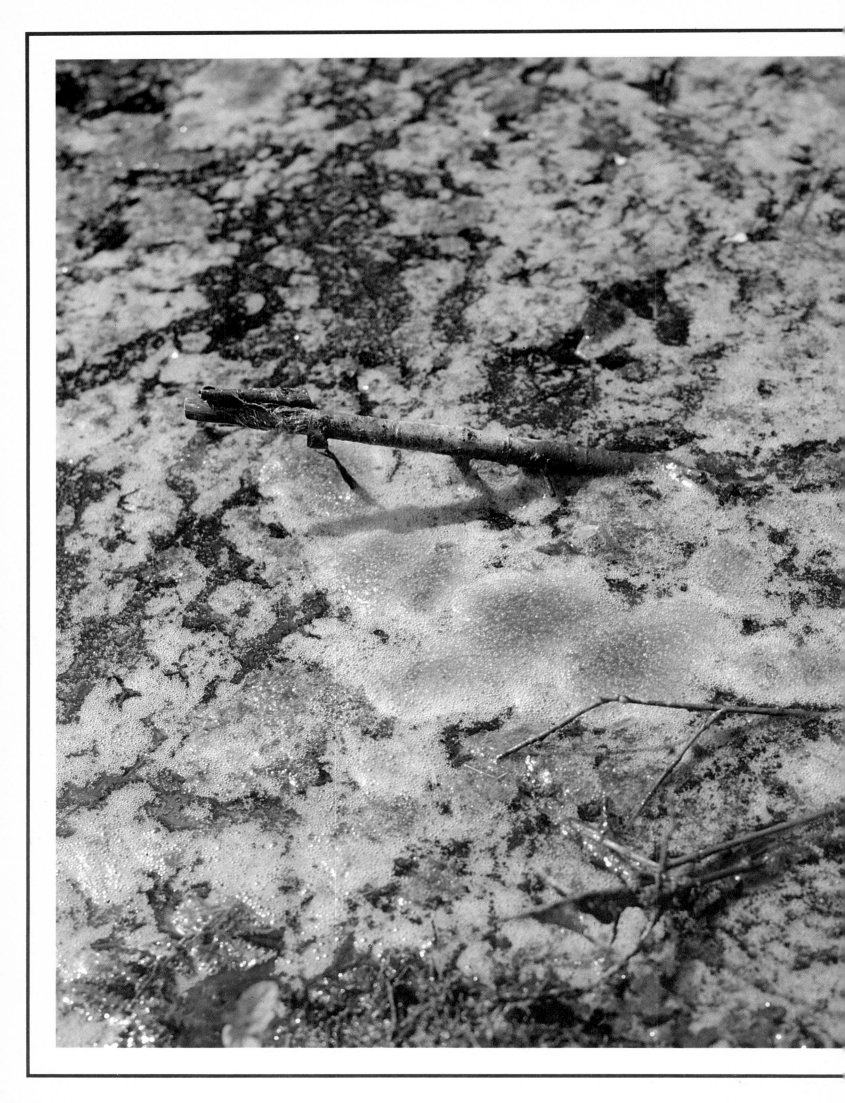

Chapter 2
From Molecules to Man

For a quarter of its history, the Earth supported no life at all. In its beginning, about 4600 million years ago, our planet condensed from a swirling cloud of interstellar dust and gas. The surface of the young Earth was far too hot to allow the existence of PROTOPLASM, the stuff of living cells. Water, a main component of protoplasm, was present only as a vapour, one among many other gases in the hot, murky atmosphere. Also, the ancient atmosphere contained no free oxygen, the gas which supports all higher forms of life. About 4000 million years ago, the Earth's surface had at last cooled sufficiently to permit water to condense and form rivers, lakes and seas. It was in water, perhaps 500 million years later still, that life first began.

A green algal scum floats on the surface of a peaty pool. Algae were among the first living cells, the microfossils of which go back 3100 million years.

The Dawn of Evolution

To find the beginnings of biological evolution, we must look for the origins of life itself. But how did life begin? First of all, it must be admitted that no one has a sure answer to this question. Because no direct evidence exists, there is plenty of room for speculation in biogenesis, as the subject is called.

Most experts, however, agree that the origins of life on Earth are to be found in the waters of ancient pools or puddles. A minority think that these first, simple forms of life were seeded there from outer space, probably enclosed and protected inside meteorites. The majority of biogenesists are more inclined to believe that planet Earth truly generated its own life, and that this arose from non-living organic matter dissolved or suspended in water.

The chemical compounds that made up this organic matter would have come from the Earth's ancient ATMOSPHERE. This consisted mainly of the gases methane, hydrogen and ammonia. Water vapour, when it condensed into a liquid on the cooling surface of the Earth, carried with it quantities of these gases in their dissolved form. At this time, the climate of the Earth would have remained very turbulent, with frequent great electrical storms. Energy was also pumping into the Earth's surface in the

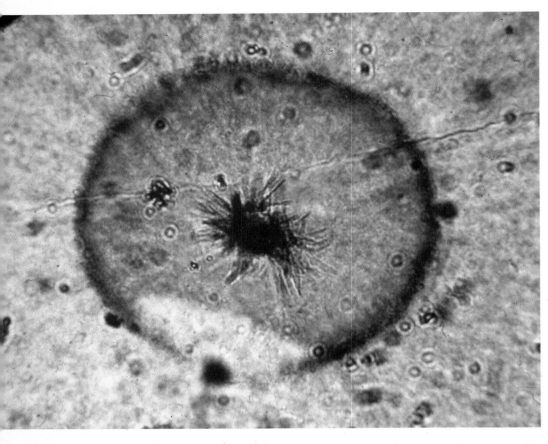

Above: A microfossil, greatly magnified, of a single-cell bluegreen alga 2000 million years old. Despite their name, bluegreen algae are more nearly related to bacteria than to other groups of algae, and they are not always bluegreen in colour!

Below: These reacted further to form long-chain polymer molecules which were able to replicate themselves forming the primeval soup.

Right: Over the next few hundred million years, the primeval soup gave rise to the first living cells.

THE ORIGIN OF LIFE ON EARTH
The most widely accepted idea is that life evolved from non-living organic matter dissolved in water. In turn, this organic matter derived from a mixture of gases in the Earth's primitive atmosphere.

Below: 4600–4000 million years ago, fierce electrical storms raged in the hot, violent atmosphere of the primitive Earth. Lethal, hard short-wave ultraviolet radiation from the Sun reached the Earth's surface.

Below: 3800 million years ago, water condensed on the Earth's cooling surface. Dissolved gases from the primitive atmosphere reacted chemically to form organic compounds.

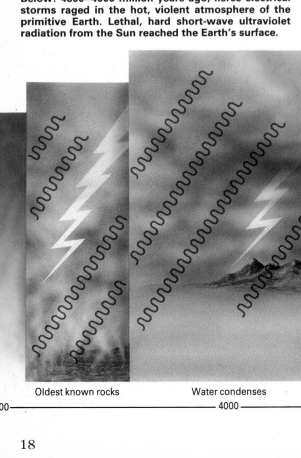

Hard ultraviolet radiation

Organic molecules

Polymer molecules

Oldest known rocks

Water condenses

First life processes

4500 — 4000 — 3800 — 3500

form of high-energy hard ULTRAVIOLET RADIA-TION from the Sun.

Such conditions would be totally inimical to life today, but they were of just the sort to cause chemical reactions to take place between the dissolved gases, to make organic chemical compounds. This idea, first put forward by the Russian scientist A. I. OPARIN, was tested in a very practical manner by the American chemists, Harold UREY and Stanley L. MILLER, in 1953.

Miller bottled up a mixture of the gases methane, hydrogen and ammonia, together with water, and shot into them electrical discharges (large sparks). The experiment was later repeated using ultraviolet radiation, with a similar result. Miller's and Urey's result, as revealed by chemical analysis of the water mixture, was that they had manufactured complex organic compounds such as AMINO ACIDS and sugars from the simple starting ingredients.

These compounds are the very ones which are the main chemical building blocks for

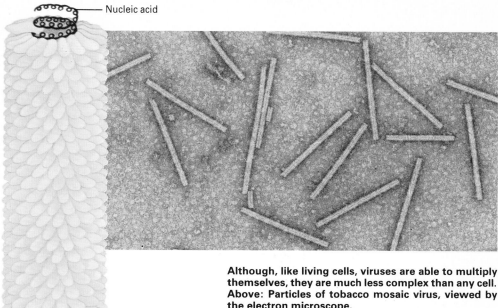

Nucleic acid

Protein sub-units

Although, like living cells, viruses are able to multiply themselves, they are much less complex than any cell. Above: Particles of tobacco mosaic virus, viewed by the electron microscope.
Left: The diagram shows how this simple virus is made up of a coat of protein enclosing a single, long molecule of nucleic acid.

the giant molecules of life. Amino acids string together to make PROTEINS, including those called ENZYMES. Sugars string together to make starch, CELLULOSE and many other plant and animal substances.

This chemical stringing together, or polymerization, would be most likely to occur when the molecules of the organic compounds were close together, as in a concentrated chemical solution – in other words, the PRIMEVAL SOUP.

Such a soup could have formed as a rock pool dried up. Another scientific idea is that small amounts of the soup could have stuck on to the surface layers of clay, which would provide a stable chemical environment.

As the size of the BIOLOGICAL POLYMERS increased, their chemical reactions with the smaller molecules became more complex. At some point, more of the polymers were being built up than were being broken down again.

Just at this point, when a population of giant biological polymers fed and grew on a diet of smaller molecules, life can be said to have begun. The life in question was a lot more ,primitive than even the simplest of living cells. But it can be compared with that of many VIRUSES, which are not much more than giant biological polymers.

Below: Paramecium is a fast-swimming, single-cell water organism of microscopic size. It is a member of the Protozoa, which includes some of the most elaborate of all living cells.

Below and right: The first cells, protected underwater from the hard ultraviolet radiation, lived anaerobic (non-oxygen-breathing) lives. Later types of green cells released oxygen into the atmosphere. This formed an ozone layer which absorbed the hard radiation and allowed life to rise to the surface.

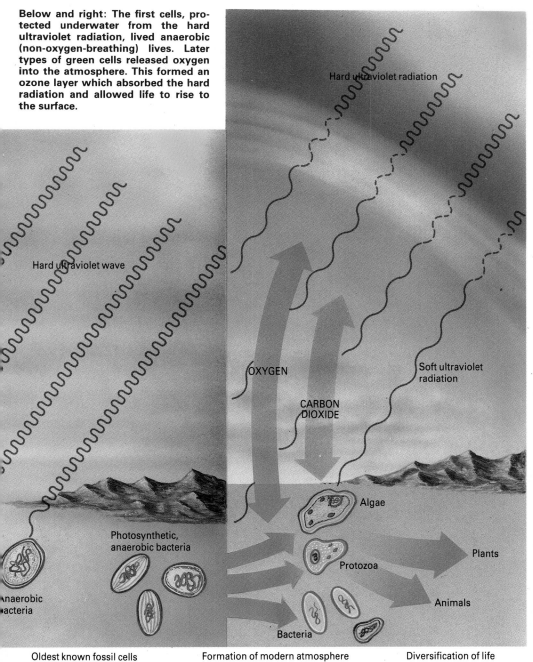

Hard ultraviolet radiation

Hard ultraviolet wave

OXYGEN

CARBON DIOXIDE

Soft ultraviolet radiation

Algae

Photosynthetic, anaerobic bacteria

Protozoa

Plants

Anaerobic bacteria

Animals

Bacteria

Oldest known fossil cells   Formation of modern atmosphere   Diversification of life
—3300————3200————2900————2000————1500————800——— Million years ago

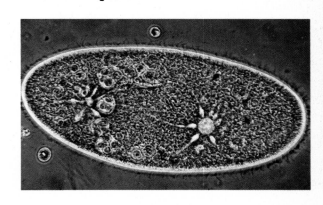

From Cells to Seaweed

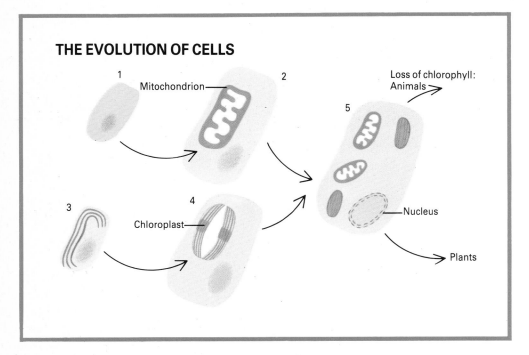

THE EVOLUTION OF CELLS

1 — Mitochondrion
2
3 — Chloroplast
4
5
Loss of chlorophyll: Animals
Nucleus
Plants

Of all the unsolved mysteries of early evolution, the greatest is that of the origin of living cells. Miller's and Urey's experiment showed how a primeval soup of giant biological molecules could have arisen. But no one has yet succeeded in making a living cell, or anything much like one, from a soup of molecules.

Even the simplest cell, such as that of a bacterium, is immensely more complicated than a polymer molecule. It is like comparing a whole factory with a single machine tool. Inside a cell, giant molecules – of DNA, enzyme proteins and so on – perform their complex and vital tasks. But they are only very small parts of the whole cell.

The fossil record does not show how the first living cells came to be formed. However, even something as microscopically small as a cell can leave a well-preserved fossil. MICROFOSSILS of single cells go back over 2000 million years, and so include the most ancient fossils of all.

Single-cell Life
The first living cells probably resembled, in their form and habit, certain mud-living BACTERIA today. They needed no free oxygen for life, and were safe from the Sun's lethal ultraviolet rays under mud and water.

Above: Living cells have undergone evolution from simpler to more complex types. The diagram shows how this could have happened. (1) and (2): One simple, bacterial cell becomes incorporated in another in a form of symbiosis. In time, the internal symbiont loses its individuality, to become a part of the larger cell called a mitochondrion. (3) and (4): In a similar way, a simple, bluegreen alga cell becomes symbiotically incorporated in a second cell, in which it evolves into a packet of chlorophyll, or chloroplast. (5): More complex algal cells formed in this way, containing both mitochondria and chloroplasts and also possessing a more elaborate nucleus, become the ancestors of both plants and animals.

Right: Life in the oceans nearly 500 million years ago was already complex and abundant. Among the largest animals were (1) nautiloids, relatives of today's squids. One is seen here capturing a large jellyfish. Animals lying on or attached to the seabed included (2) and (3) brachiopods, a very ancient group of two-shelled animals, and (4) and (5) extinct relatives of starfishes and sea urchins. Animals living in colonies included, then as now, (6) corals and (7) bryozoans. Another extinct relative of starfishes (8) is seen clinging to one of the bryozoan colonies. Active seabed crawlers included various trilobites (9), (10) and (11) although one of these has rolled itself up into a ball. The only large plants (12) were seaweeds.

In this primitive form, life must have continued for many hundreds of millions of years. Eventually, it gave rise to the first plant-like organisms. These were still microscopic single cells, but their existence led to the most profound change in the Earth's surface environment, which in turn brought life to the Earth's surface.

The first plant-like cells, like those of today, contained CHLOROPHYLL. By means of this magic green pigment, they built up the carbon dioxide dissolved in their watery home into the complex carbon substances of their own cells. In doing so, they also split water into hydrogen and oxygen, using up the hydrogen but releasing the oxygen into the atmosphere.

Over a further great stretch of time, this free oxygen accumulated until it reached the concentration we breathe today, that is, about one-fifth of the total atmosphere. But long before this concentration was attained, some of the oxygen, high up in the atmosphere, had been converted by ultraviolet radiation into the gas, OZONE. The ozone layer so formed then absorbed the high-energy radiation, allowing only long-wave softer, less harmful ultraviolet rays to reach the Earth's surface.

Radiation of Life
If the first great step in evolution was the formation of living cells, then the second was the expansion of life, from its submerged, muddy niche, into a rich variety of forms which took advantage of the new, more benevolent surface conditions. The earliest, bacteria-like cells gave rise to a range of more complex cells resembling

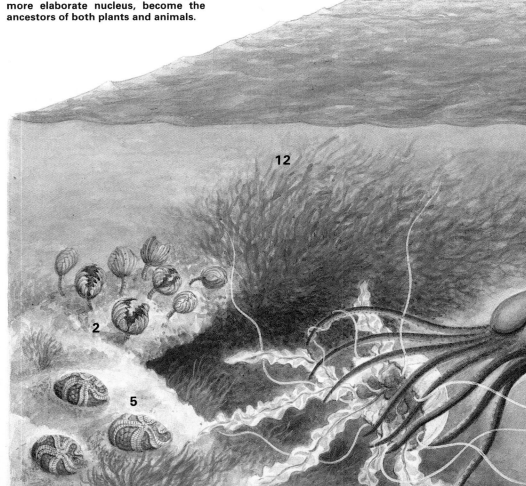

12
2
5

Right: A living sponge on the floor of the Red Sea. Sponges are among the simplest of all multicellular animals, consisting of only a few kinds of living cells.

those of today's ALGAE, familiar as green scums on ponds, and also as seaweeds.

Whereas many algae in pond scums are single cells, seaweeds are many-celled forms of life. The early seaweeds were the first life forms to reach a considerable size. Indeed, some giant kelps of today can be a hundred metres (328 ft) or more long.

Parallel with the development of these early plants came the beginnings of animal life. At first, this too was microscopic in size. Some single-cell algae lost their chlorophyll. They could no longer make their own food, so absorbed it instead from their surrounding environment. In this way arose not only such single-celled 'animals' as the amoebas, but also the earliest kind of FUNGI.

The first multi-celled animals of visible size would have resembled the sponges and jellyfishes of today. Compared with all other animals, sponges are very simply organized, being built up of only a few different kinds of cells. Jellyfishes and their relatives are rather more elaborately organized, with two separate layers of cells, performing different duties on the inside and on the outside of the body. The vast majority of all animals higher than these have much more complex, three-layered bodies containing great numbers of different types of cells.

Right: A fossil sea urchin. Echinoderms, the great and ancient group of animals to which sea urchins belong, have left excellently preserved fossils throughout the ages. Their hard, chalky bodies are among the most suitable in the animal kingdom for the fossilization process.

Below: A trilobite fossil dating from about 390 million years ago. Trilobites were very numerous arthropod inhabitants of ancient seas. Their armoured bodies left a long and varied record in the rocks.

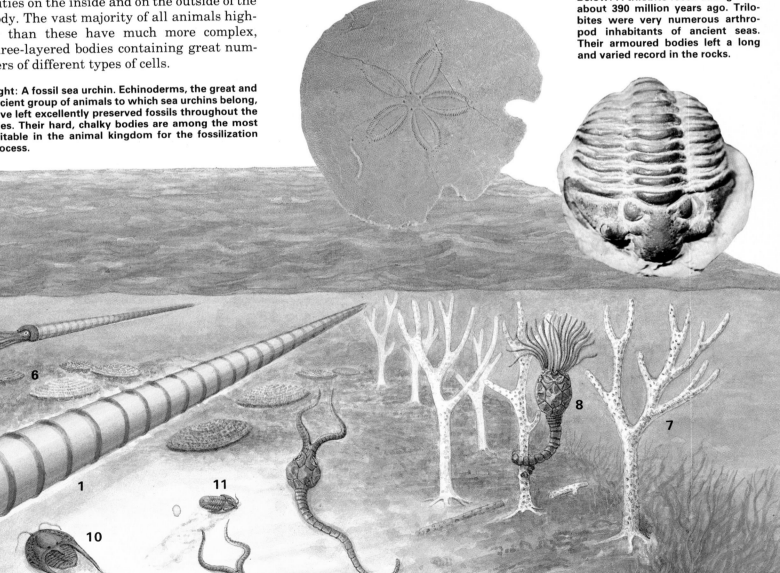

Life Conquers the Oceans

Five hundred million years ago, the oceans already teemed with a life which included members of every one of the thirty or so major groups of animals that exist today.

As well as sponges and jellyfishes, there were corals and sea anemones, many kinds of worms, and relatives of modern starfishes, squids, snails, spiders and crabs – to name only some of the most familiar types. All these are INVERTEBRATES, or animals without backbones. The earliest VERTEBRATES, or backboned animals, were also present, as fishes, in the waters of DEVONIAN seas.

Devonian Sealife

Then, as now, many of the smallest of sea creatures were members of the plankton, mixed animal and plant life which drifted and floated in the surface layers of the oceans. Small though each member might be, the plankton, living in vast areas right across the oceans, made up a huge biomass, or quantity of life, upon which ultimately depended the lives of all other, larger animals.

These larger animals notably included the

TRILOBITES and the sea scorpions, or eurypterids, which were members of the great group of the ARTHROPODS, or joint-legged animals. Trilobites were somewhat similar in form to the horseshoe crab, whereas the sea scorpions were ARACHNIDS, giant relatives of spiders and scorpions up to two metres (over six feet) in length.

The first fishes to leave fossils were small, jawless vertebrates. They scooped up food from the bottom mud into their slit-like mouths and their heads were extensively armoured with bone. Their modern descendants, the soft-bodied lampreys and hagfishes, which live mostly as PARASITES on other fishes, bear little obvious resemblance, apart from their jawless mouth, to their bony ancestors.

Later in the Devonian Period (395–345 million years ago) appeared a much wider range of fishes which in general bore a greater resemblance to today's fishes. They included early sharks and BONY FISHES, which have left many modern descendants. The sharks, rays and their relatives are remarkable vertebrates in that their skel-

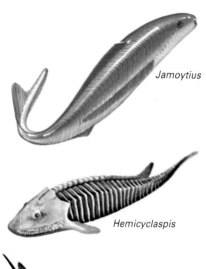

Jamoytius

Hemicyclaspis

Pteraspis

Left: Jawless fishes are the oldest known backboned animals. *Hemicyclaspis* and *Pteraspis* were heavily-armoured mud grubbers. *Jamoytius* was nearer the direct line of ancestry of today's lampreys and hagfishes, and, like them, had an unarmoured body. All were small fishes.

Dinichthys

The Devonian seas, 360 million years ago, were ruled by a varied population of fishes, some of which were large and ferocious animals. Most fearsome of all was *Dinichthys*, largest of the placoderm fishes, a group that later became extinct after failing in competition with the early sharks. The first sharks and rays are represented here by *Cladoselache*, a small, fast-swimming shark, and *Aellopos*, a bottom-dwelling ancestor of modern rays.

eton contains no bone: this has been replaced entirely by a hard, rather glassy cartilage.

The bony fishes, as their name implies, have kept their bony skeletons. One group of bony fishes, the teleosts, are the greatest evolutionary success among water vertebrates. Ninety-nine out of a hundred fishes still living today are teleosts. The bodies of these fishes show an immense range of adaptations for life in water – as great as that of reptiles, birds and mammals for life on the land.

Placoderms

Some of the early sharks and bony fishes were fairly large fast-moving fishes, but much larger and more dangerous still were members of a group that did not survive, the placoderms.

The largest placoderms were great predators up to nine metres (30 ft) in length: heavy-bodied, with huge bony heads and gaping jaws. The skull of a placoderm, unlike that of any living vertebrate, was, like its lower jaw, hinged so that it could be moved up and down. Undoubtedly, this gave a placoderm a very large gape but, since the whole group became extinct soon after the Devonian Period, perhaps this was not such a good design feature after all.

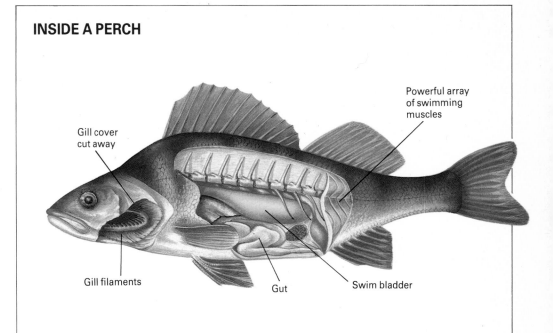

INSIDE A PERCH

Gill cover cut away

Powerful array of swimming muscles

Gill filaments

Gut

Swim bladder

A perch, an advanced representative of the teleost fishes, the dominant backboned inhabitants of marine and fresh waters. Among its many refined adaptations to the aquatic life is its swim bladder, by which it precisely controls its vertical movements, or poises at a particular level in the water. This hydrostatic organ has descended from a primitive lung of the kind still possessed by such archaic fishes as the lungfishes and the Nile bichir.

Cladoselache

Aellopos

A swift, modern ocean predator – the mako shark.

The First Land Plants

Zosterophyllum

Cooksonia

Of the higher forms of life, plants were the first to colonize the land. Until land plants were widespread, animals could not have ventured far from water because they depend on plants, directly or indirectly, for food.

A typical land plant is something green that projects, more or less upright, from the soil into the air. This description, oversimplified as it is, reveals two major differences between the early water plants and the early land plants.

For an aquatic plant such as a seaweed to evolve into a land plant of any considerable size, it would need to develop strength and stiffness to overcome the pull of gravity and replace the buoyancy of water. At the same time, it would have to develop some way of preventing loss of water from its tissues to the air. A stranded seaweed, without this protection, soon shrivels and hardens.

Living Ancestors

We can often find living evidence of past evolutionary progress because ancient groups of living organisms tend to persist, even if in much fewer numbers and varieties.

In widely scattered parts of the southern hemisphere live the last remnants – three species – of the most ancient group of true land plants. The psilotales, as they are called, are the size of ferns but lack such fern-like refinements as roots and well-developed leaves.

However, their narrow, aerial stems, which spring upright from creeping under-

Below: *Psilotum* is a primitive land plant growing in a few tropical locations. In Hawaii, it colonizes lava flows and is known as the Moa plant.

Right: Plants of the coal forests, together with their fossils. Some, such as the smaller horsetail and the tree fern, are similar to plants still living today. The seed ferns and giant horsetails and clubmosses, on the other hand, have long disappeared.

1 Small horsetail

Small seed fern

1

ground stems, are well adapted for life out of water. They contain woody tubes or vessels which not only stiffen the stems but also serve to conduct water from underground to all parts of the plant. Other vessels conduct liquid foodstuffs, and the presence of these specialized vessels explains the term vascular plants, of which the psilotales are the oldest and most primitive survivors.

Missing Plant Links

It might well be objected that such plants do not look much like seaweeds. Is there a MISSING LINK between the two types?

The rare psilotales are, indeed, the most primitive living vascular plants, but a look around any garden or woodland will reveal many small, non-vascular land plants. The mosses, without any VASCULAR TISSUES, are unable to grow to any considerable size, but in their small way they are a very successful group, as their commonness shows.

Mosses and their close relatives, the liverworts, also lack the outer skin, or cuticle, that protects the leaves and young stems of vascular plants from water loss. For this reason, the mosses and liverworts are more dependent on a watery environment. Landlocked mosses get their water from rain and dew, but many liverworts need to live partly submerged, as on the banks of streams.

The plant body, or thallus, of a liverwort consists of irregularly-shaped green lobes, which are held to the bank it grows on by rootlike RHIZOIDS (which are, however, much simpler than true roots). The liverwort reproduces itself by the fertilization of an egg with a motile sperm and the sperm needs water to be able to swim to the egg.

But this description fits equally well a small seaweed such as a green alga of coastal waters. Perhaps, in the liverwort, we have the nearest thing to a missing link between the original water plants and the plants that moved on to the land.

PLANTS OF THE COAL FORESTS

Ulva

Above: How did land-dwelling plants evolve from ancient aquatic plants? For lack of fossil evidence, this question has never been answered. However, the two small living plants shown provide at least a partial answer. *Ulva*, the sea lettuce, is a small green seaweed. The very similar liverwort is a freshwater plant related to the mosses, which are land plants.

5 *Lepidodendron*, a gigantic clubmoss

4 *Calamites*, a giant horsetail

3 *Psaronius*, a tree fern

2 *Medullosa*, a seed fern

The First Land Animals

Even before Devonian times, some joint-legged, sea-scorpion-like creatures could have emerged from the oceans, lakes and rivers to take up a life on the shore. They would not have strayed far from the water's edge because little plant food was to be found inland. However, in general they would have been adapted quite well for life out of water. Their small size and rigid outer skeleton solved, or avoided, the gravity problem. They breathed air with gills shielded from drying out – perhaps similar to those of modern scorpions.

Such a description, while convincing enough, is almost totally speculative because no fossils of such early land arthropods survive. Even the related INSECTS, which arose later on and eventually diversified into a vast range of land-living invertebrates, have left a disappointingly small record in the rocks. Rare, well-preserved insect fossils include those in sediments and those in which the insect is preserved whole, trapped in a hardened, transparent tree resin called amber.

Land insects first appeared in Devonian times. In the age of the great coal swamps that followed, they radiated into many forms. Among the scanty fossils of these early insects, the most startling specimens are those of giant dragonflies with a wing-span of nearly 75 cm (about 2½ feet). These, the largest insects ever to have lived, became extinct at the time of the early dinosaurs at the beginning of the Mesozoic Era. Indeed, none of the first insect groups survived into our own times. Fossils of modern insects, together with those of many other invertebrates, go back no earlier than the Tertiary Period, 60 million years ago.

Below: A panorama of life in the swampy coal forests, 300 million years ago. Early land animals include a giant dragonfly with a 68-cm (27-in) wing-span, and a bulky early amphibian carnivore, *Eryops*. Many extinct trees are also shown (see pages 23–24 to identify some of them).

Vertebrates on Land

Much larger even than the giant dragonflies were their contemporaries, the first four-legged land animals or tetrapods. These 'walking fishes', unlike the early land invertebrates, left behind a wealth of fossil evidence. They also left descendants that have survived until the present day.

In sluggish, turbid inland waters of Africa, South America and Australia live the lungfishes. In periods of drought, these doughty creatures last out the dry conditions encased in clay, breathing air through a pore at the clay surface. Unlike a typical land animal, a lungfish has no legs. But among lungfish ancestors are fishes with very leglike fins.

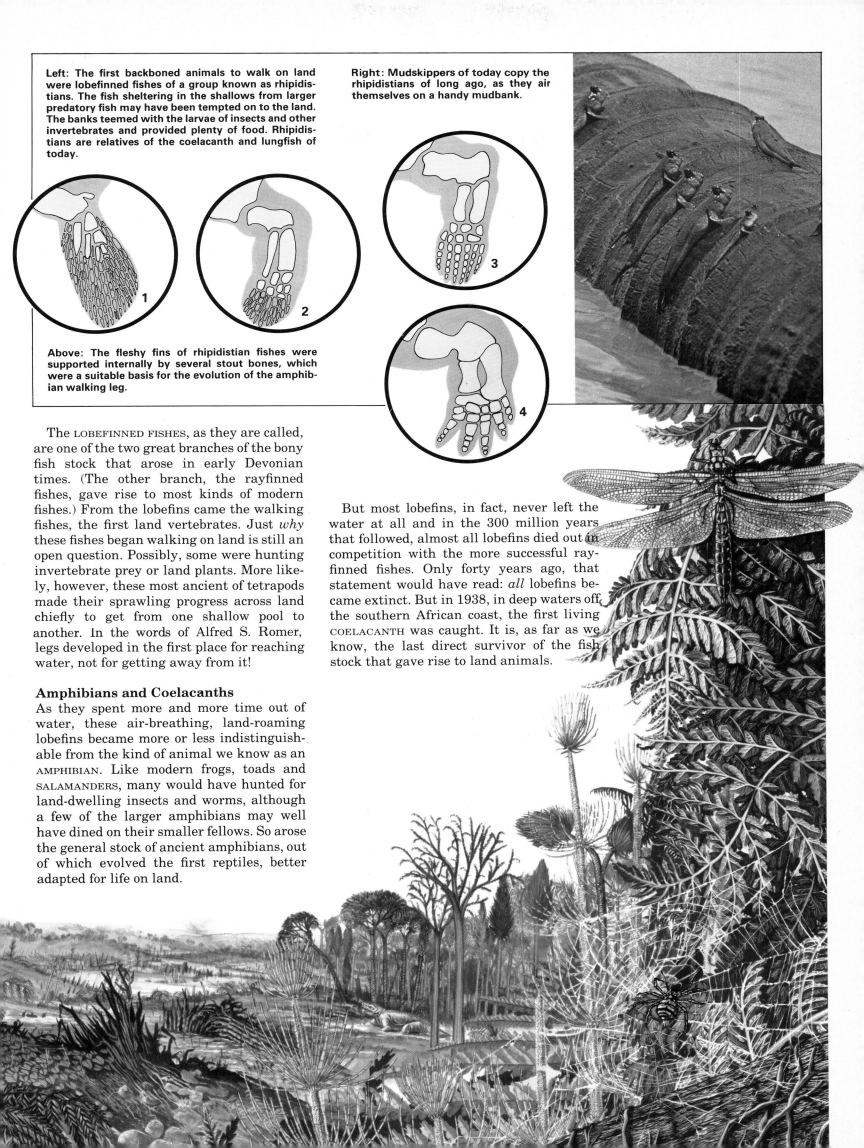

Left: The first backboned animals to walk on land were lobefinned fishes of a group known as rhipidistians. The fish sheltering in the shallows from larger predatory fish may have been tempted on to the land. The banks teemed with the larvae of insects and other invertebrates and provided plenty of food. Rhipidistians are relatives of the coelacanth and lungfish of today.

Right: Mudskippers of today copy the rhipidistians of long ago, as they air themselves on a handy mudbank.

Above: The fleshy fins of rhipidistian fishes were supported internally by several stout bones, which were a suitable basis for the evolution of the amphibian walking leg.

The LOBEFINNED FISHES, as they are called, are one of the two great branches of the bony fish stock that arose in early Devonian times. (The other branch, the rayfinned fishes, gave rise to most kinds of modern fishes.) From the lobefins came the walking fishes, the first land vertebrates. Just *why* these fishes began walking on land is still an open question. Possibly, some were hunting invertebrate prey or land plants. More likely, however, these most ancient of tetrapods made their sprawling progress across land chiefly to get from one shallow pool to another. In the words of Alfred S. Romer, legs developed in the first place for reaching water, not for getting away from it!

Amphibians and Coelacanths

As they spent more and more time out of water, these air-breathing, land-roaming lobefins became more or less indistinguishable from the kind of animal we know as an AMPHIBIAN. Like modern frogs, toads and SALAMANDERS, many would have hunted for land-dwelling insects and worms, although a few of the larger amphibians may well have dined on their smaller fellows. So arose the general stock of ancient amphibians, out of which evolved the first reptiles, better adapted for life on land.

But most lobefins, in fact, never left the water at all and in the 300 million years that followed, almost all lobefins died out in competition with the more successful rayfinned fishes. Only forty years ago, that statement would have read: *all* lobefins became extinct. But in 1938, in deep waters off the southern African coast, the first living COELACANTH was caught. It is, as far as we know, the last direct survivor of the fish stock that gave rise to land animals.

The Rule of Reptiles

Right: The first reptiles to become dominant on land were, strangely enough, those recognized as mammal-like. Among these was *Edaphosaurus*, a plant-eater of 275 million years ago. Like other large reptiles of its time, it sported a sail-like structure, which may have acted alternately as a cooling fin and a heating surface, and helped it to control its body temperature.

A pterosaur

Below: About 200 million years ago, the early mammal-like reptiles gave way to the more versatile dinosaurs, the 'terrible lizards'. This scene from the middle of the dinosaurs' 130-million-year reign shows the carnivore *Allosaurus*, living up to its name of leaping lizard, in hot pursuit of a smaller dinosaur relative, *Ornitholestes* (bird lizard). In the middle-ground, a large herbivore, *Camptosaurus* (bent lizard), dines off cycad fronds, while a pterosaur (winged reptile) soars high overhead. Browsing from more distant treetops is the largest of all dinosaurs, *Brachiosaurus* (arm lizard) – who was a monster weighing 50 tonnes (49·2 tons). Cropping in the background is *Stegosaurus* (plate reptile), a huge armoured dinosaur.

The first reptiles evolved from amphibians about 280 million years ago. Their fossils show them to have been clumsy beasts, no remarkable advance on their amphibian forebears. But these animals had perfected one great evolutionary invention – the land egg. This has a thick, protective shell that retains vital moisture and contains a large supply of yolk food for the developing reptile embryo. Probably, then as now, most mother reptiles took little or no care of their eggs once they had laid them – other than covering them up with soil, perhaps – but a young reptile hatches at a much more advanced stage of development than the amphibian tadpole, and so is less likely to be snapped up as a tidbit by a passing predator.

All of the earliest kinds of reptile long ago died out, superseded by more versatile and

Brachiosaurus

Camptosaurus

Ornitholestes

active creatures. Among their immediate descendants, however, one group has plodded on through the ages, diversifying a little here and there, but remaining for the most part unchanged. Safe under their massive armour, the tortoises and turtles are among the most conservative – and also the most successful – of living reptiles.

The Age of Reptiles

The livelier successors to the earliest reptiles were the first RULING REPTILES. Small and lizard-like, they were the forerunners of a great reptile empire which lasted for another 140 million years and spanned the Mesozoic Era. The ruling reptiles radiated into every major natural niche and so demonstrated how much fitter they were than the amphibians to inherit the Earth. Freed from dependence on water, many became inhabitants of forests, open plains and even deserts. Others, however, chose to go back to the water, developing bodies shaped like fish or sea serpents. Yet others took to the air, some becoming gigantic living gliders. Most famous of all are the DINOSAURS, which included not only the most terrifying flesh-eaters ever to live on land, but also the

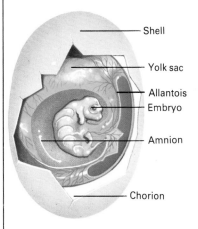

INSIDE A REPTILE EGG

- Shell
- Yolk sac
- Allantois
- Embryo
- Amnion
- Chorion

The reptiles' greatest invention for conquering the land was their egg. This does not dry up on land, as an amphibian's egg would, because its vital moisture is retained by the tough, leathery shell. Within its double layer of membranes – chorion and amnion – the reptile embryo is well shielded from mechanical shock and from temperature fluctuations. The egg's yolk sac provides food, which is carried to the embryo through blood vessels. A third membrane, the allantois, collects body wastes excreted by the embryo.

largest land beasts of all, vast plant-eaters weighing up to 50 tonnes.

Not all these remarkable reptiles lived at the same time. Rather, they followed one another in waves. Fairly early on in the Age of Reptiles came selection for sheer bulk, when evolution produced such ponderous monsters as the *Apatosaurus* and the *Brachiosaurus*.

Rather later came dinosaurs whose success lay in their armoured impregnability, such as cumbersome beasts like *Stegosaurus*. So far, brain and speed had definitely not been at a high premium, but later large dinosaurs were faster and brainier. These included such great carnivores as *Gorgosaurus* and *Tyrannosaurus*, and hugely armoured but agiles herbivores, some, such as *Triceratops*, with great horns.

But these were only the largest and heaviest dinosaurs. Many other successful types, such as the duckbills and ostrich-like dinosaurs, were of middling size. The smallest dinosaurs were no bigger than chickens.

All these and many more ruling reptiles flourished, waned and finally became extinct. In the end, even this great and various group of animals lacked the versatility to withstand geographical and climatic changes. But among the less spectacular of these reptiles are to be found the ancestors of many living animals. Crocodiles, like turtles, form a durable group that has changed little since its early days. Lizards and snakes are rather more adventurous descendants. But the greatest evolutionary success of the ruling reptiles is a type of animal that has outdistanced its ancestors in every respect except size and ferocity – the BIRD.

Allosaurus

Stegosaurus

Left: Fossils of very early birds are extremely rare but that of *Archaeopteryx*, a contemporary of the dinosaurs on the previous page, is so well preserved that it is possible to reconstruct the animal almost completely. *Archaeopteryx* was a true bird, but only just. It had a bird's feathers and could fly, if rather weakly. Its numerous teeth, tree-climbing wing claws, long bony tail and general body shape were, however, still reptilian.

Birds, or Feathered Reptiles

Even the two largest and strongest of living birds, the ostrich and emu, being feathered and quite toothless, would remind very few people of a dinosaur. As for smaller birds such as the wren, robin and crow – what reptile could ever fly as they do?

However, a glance at a bird's leg will show that it is narrow and scaly and terminates in a grasping foot with clawed toes – very like a dinosaur's leg and foot. The first birds, like those of today, had feathers and could fly, but they also had a beak filled with typical reptilian teeth. The earliest birds could not actually have been good fliers, lacking the great bony breast keel, or sternum, of modern birds, and the big wing muscles attached to this keel. Probably they flapped heavily from tree to tree, to escape their enemies and to search for tree foods such as berries and other fruits.

Animals that live in trees rarely leave complete, well-preserved fossils. Their bodies, after a predatory attack, are much more likely to come to earth in bits! A bird's bones, being delicate structures filled with air spaces, are particularly unlikely to fossilize well. So it is not surprising that our knowledge of extinct birds has to be based on a mere handful of fossils.

Archaeopteryx & Co.

The oldest of known birds are *Archaeopteryx* and *Archaeornis*, which lived about 140 million years ago, contemporaries of the huge plant-eating dinosaurs. They were truly feathered reptiles. Not only did they have reptilian teeth, but their tails, although feather-covered, were reptilian in their length and boniness. Even their feathers, seemingly unlike a reptile's scaly covering, were actually a development of those scales. Certainly they were weak fliers. Like the modern hoatzin, a bird living in trees overhanging swamps, they clambered about from branch to branch with the aid of wing claws.

The pelvic bones of these archaic birds give the best clue to their particular origins. This pelvis is of the same general shape as that of such dinosaurs as the duckbills and the three-horned *Triceratops*. This does not mean that birds are descended from these dinosaurs, but that both have common ancestors among the early reptiles.

Modern Birds

Late in the Age of Reptiles, the successors of the first birds took on various forms. Some became better fliers whereas others lost the power of flight altogether and became fish-hunting swimmers. Still later flightless types followed the evolutionary tendency to hugeness, but their bones have been preserved whereas perhaps those of smaller contemporary birds have not. The fossil record is at best sketchy.

The wonderful variety of bird life today shows that despite the lack of fossil evidence, there can be no doubt of the great success of birds as an animal group. Modern birds differ from their remote ancestors in several important respects. Not only their wing muscles, but also their larger eyes and brains, and their complex behaviour patterns are adaptations for a life of nesting and migratory flight.

Above: This young hoatzin resembles the long extinct *Archaeopteryx*, but no other living bird, in one important feature – its wing claws, with which it clambers about the tree branches overhanging rivers and swamps in South America.

Below: Feathers help a bird to fly and also serve to keep it warm. Like the hair of mammals, feathers evolved from the scales of reptiles – all three are made of the protein keratin. Under the microscope, however, feathers are seen to be much more elaborate structures than hair or scales, with many interlocking barbs and barbules.

Barbules

Barbs

A modern, strong flier – the striated caracara of South
America. This long-legged, falcon-like bird is probably
on the lookout for carrion.

The Mammal Story

Above: The first true mammals were small creatures living in the shadow of much larger reptiles, as far back as early dinosaurs. This reconstruction of *Pantothere*, which lived 200 million years ago, shows its primitive, shrew-like appearance. But probably, like the more old-fashioned platypus and *Echidna*, *Pantothere* would have been an egg-laying mammal.

All through the Age of Reptiles, mammals were also fairly abundant. Smaller and less conspicuous than their reptile overlords, they would have used their extra nimbleness mostly for keeping out of harm's way. With carnivorous dinosaurs around, increased size and visibility, unaccompanied by armour and ferocity, would have been a positive disadvantage!

The fossils of MAMMAL-LIKE REPTILES, ancestors of these small Mesozoic mammals, have been found dating from the Permian Period, well before the rise of the ruling reptiles. It is unlikely that these bulkier, fiercely fanged mammal ancestors had such typical mammal traits as hair, warm blood and milk glands. But their legs, instead of sprawling sideways like those of amphibians and sluggish reptiles, were gathered under their body in the manner of the swifter mammals.

The dinosaurs came on to the evolutionary scene, and these early progenitors of mammals disappeared from it, leaving behind only the much smaller, shrew-like mammals that escaped notice throughout the Age of

Right: The way in which animals and plants are distributed worldwide can be explained by the drifting apart of continents during the past 200 million years. This is also roughly the span of the Age of Mammals, and the distribution of these animals is a particularly good indication of continental drift. The earliest mammals arose when the continents were bunched together as the vast land mass of Pangaea. The first continent to separate widely was Australasia, and it is there that the most archaic of living mammals, the egg-laying platypus and *Echidna*, are found. Australasia also has the great majority of the marsupials, another very ancient group, although a few of these mammals are found in the American continent. Similarities between the fauna of East Africa and India — such as buffaloes — are explained by the Indian sub-continent having separated from Africa and joined on to Asia.

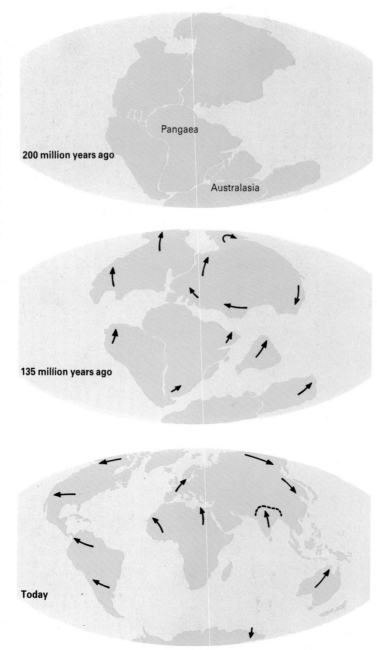

200 million years ago

Pangaea

Australasia

135 million years ago

Today

Reptiles. When, in their turn, the dinosaurs became extinct, a fertile world awaited the expansion of the mammals. And expand they did into a multitude of contrasted forms, so that by 50 million years ago they were already the dominant animals on the Earth's land surface.

Adaptability and Intelligence

Mammals were able to succeed where the reptiles had failed because they were more adaptable to change. When the climate became colder, a cold-blooded reptile, whatever its size and muscle power, became more inactive. In severe cold, its eggs, unattended and perhaps unshielded, died without hatching. A warm-blooded mammal, insulated by the blanket of air trapped within its hairy coat, could remain active even in severe cold. Its newborn young, well fed with mother's milk, stayed safe and snug in their warm nest or burrow.

Compare any group of mammals with any group of reptiles, and further major differences become obvious. The mammals are much more aware of one another as indi-

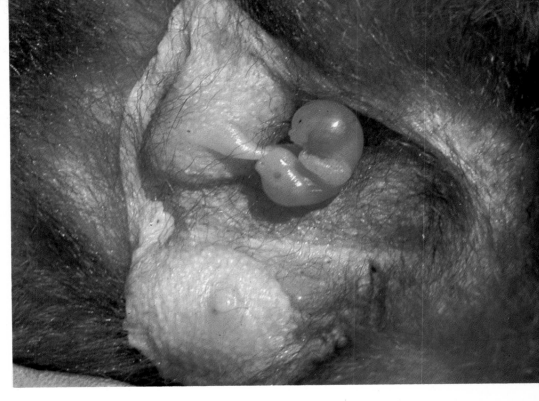

Above: Marsupials have taken one large step farther away from reptiles than the egg-laying mammals. Their young are brought into the world at a very early stage of development. They are then nurtured and protected inside the mother's pouch until they are old enough to take care of themselves. The pouch of this Australian brush-tailed opossum has been opened to show its newborn baby, less than 2 cm (¾ inch) long, attached to the teat where it will remain until much more fully developed.

Left: Like the brush-tailed opossum, the kinkajou is often to be seen hanging upside-down in its native trees. There, however, the resemblance ends, because the kinkajou is a placental mammal. The mother kinkajou retains her young inside her body for a longer period, nourishing them there with food substances from her own blood. Newborn kinkajous are much larger and more fully developed than newborn opossums.

viduals. They are truly family animals, or herd animals, whereas reptiles are not. During their nursing period, infant mammals remain close to their mother and to one another. In many mammals, this has led to the development of play and learning, and a corresponding further increase in intelligence.

Mammal Variety

Like birds, mammals are active, warm-blooded creatures. But birds – allowing for their wide variety of size and colour – are mostly very similar under their feathers, whereas mammals' bodies differ greatly in design and function.

Most archaic of living mammals are the platypus and *Echidna* of Australasia, which lay eggs and suckle their newly hatched young with primitive, teat-less milk glands.

More distinctively mammalian than these evolutionary leftovers are the pouched mammals or MARSUPIALS, most of which also live in Australasia, although a few opossums live in South America. The marsupial young is brought into the world mammal-fashion, but as a tiny creature at a stage of development corresponding to a human foetus only a month or so old.

By far the most numerous and widespread of living mammals are the PLACENTAL MAMMALS, named after the internal organ that nourishes the unborn young during its prolonged stay in the womb.

But why such fundamental differences between groups of living mammals? Surely, the platypus, *Echidna*, wombat and wallaby should long ago have disappeared after failing to compete with the more modern placentals? The last question contains its own answer. Egg-laying and marsupial mammals have survived only because they remained in total geographical isolation from placental would-be rivals for hundreds of millions of years.

Evolution of mammals

Perissodactyls
Carnivores
Proboscids
Ancestral herbivores
Creodonts
Artiodactyls
Primates
Edentates
Reptiles
TRIASSIC
Bats
Rodents
CRETACEOUS
Mesozoic mammals
Insectivores
Lagomorphs
Cetaceans
Monotremes
Marsupials
TERTIARY

The Ancestry of Man

Among the varied mammal populations inhabiting the Earth 45 million years ago were those of small, rather unspecialized tree-dwellers. Ranging in size and appearance from shrew-like to squirrel-like, they were unremarkable creatures when compared with many larger EOCENE mammals. These early PRIMATES (the name of the family which includes man), like birds and other tree-dwellers of the past, left very few fossils, so that the remote ancestry of such living mammals as lemurs, monkeys, apes and human beings is still very hazy.

From time to time a primate would leave the trees and take up a ground life. It is possible that this generally happened when it became too bulky for swinging about in the branches with complete safety. An early example is a fossil lemur the size of a man. More recently the gorilla, largest of the living apes, has descended from the trees for the same reason.

In widespread parts of the world, 14 million years ago, lived an ape-like creature about the size of a chimpanzee. From its middling size, *RAMAPITHECUS*, as it is now called, could have been either a tree-dweller or a ground-dweller. If the latter, then possibly it could have walked upright, at least, if forced to. Its teeth, although still quite ape-like, were also in other ways quite man-like. *Ramapithecus* is, as far as we know, the first HOMINID, or man's oldest direct ancestor.

Australopithecines

After *Ramapithecus* follows a great gap in the fossil record of man-like primates. This record is slowly being completed by ANTHROPOLOGISTS working in EAST AFRICA, where most fossils of early man have been found. The most ancient of fossils adjudged definitely more like men than apes are recent African finds dating from about five million

Above: A common tree shrew of Asian forests. These small mammals are very similar both to insectivores, such as the true shrews, and to primates, the group to which man belongs. They may well represent the most primitive stage of primate evolution.

Below: *Dryopithecus* is the most likely candidate for the ancestor of modern apes. It lived at about the same time as *Ramapithecus* (see right) who was man's oldest direct ancestor.

THE ANCESTRY OF MAN

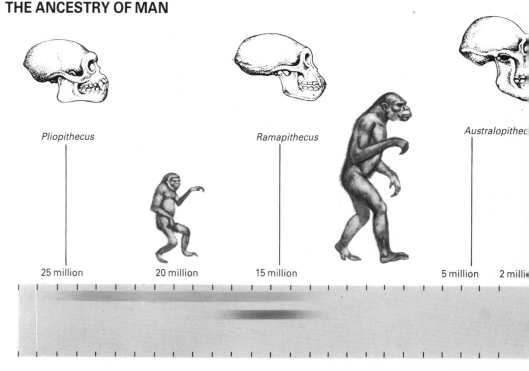

Pliopithecus

Ramapithecus

Australopithec

25 million   20 million   15 million   5 million   2 milli

years ago, that is, nine million years after *Ramapithecus*.

These fossils are recognized as those of bipeds called AUSTRALOPITHECINES. In the last half-century many australopithecine fossils have been uncovered in Africa, the youngest dating from about one and three quarter million years ago. Only a metre or so (about four feet) in height, these creatures walked and ran upright, but their skulls and facial features were more like those of a chimpanzee. During their three million (or more) years in Africa, they invented stone tools ranging from simple hand-held pebbles to sharp-edged stone cutters.

Homo at Last

Australopithecines are judged too physically unlike human beings to merit the name *Homo*. Fossils of the first primates to be awarded this title have been dated from the end of the australopithecine period. *Homo erectus*, to give the first human being its full name, was first known colloquially as 'The Ape Man of Java'.

Homo erectus roamed the Earth for at least one million years, making such important discoveries as the control of fire for heating and cooking. In time, it gave rise to modern man, *Homo sapiens*. A few scattered fossils of modern man date from as long ago as 250,000 years, and when *Homo sapiens* appears on the scene in greater numbers, 150,000 to 60,000 years ago, it is not as one type but at least two. The lower-browed of these 'ancient moderns' is *Homo sapiens neanderthalensis*, or Neanderthal Man. Often mistaken for a shambling ancestor, Neanderthal Man is really more a cousin of modern man, with whom it interbred. It probably disappeared about 30,000 years ago, leaving only its loftier-browed cousin, *Homo sapiens sapiens*, to inherit the Earth.

Below: Walking upright, man's ancestors advance through time. More than 20 million years ago lived *Pliopithecus*, a small primate who could walk bipedally – but it was an ancestor of the gibbons rather than of man. About 14 million years ago appeared *Ramapithecus*, the first primate to resemble man more than the apes. A gap of nine million years followed before the first appearance of *Australopithecus*, a creature with a very human body but a chimpanzee-like head and face. *Australopithecus* ruled for at least three and a half million years before being supplanted by the first species of man's own genus, *Homo erectus*. Descendants of *Homo erectus* included Neanderthal Man, who probably disappeared about 30,000 years ago, and modern man.

Above: A scene near Lake Rudolf, Northern Kenya, two and a half million years ago. A group of the man-like primates called australopithecines are making a rough camp. One carries sticks, but not for a fire because the art of firemaking has yet to be learned. Others use pebbles and sticks as tools for hunting and killing prey and here to construct a clumsy windbreak. The sturdy form of these hominids show them to be of the species *Australopithecus boisei* as distinct from the slenderer *Australopithecus africanus*, also living at that time.

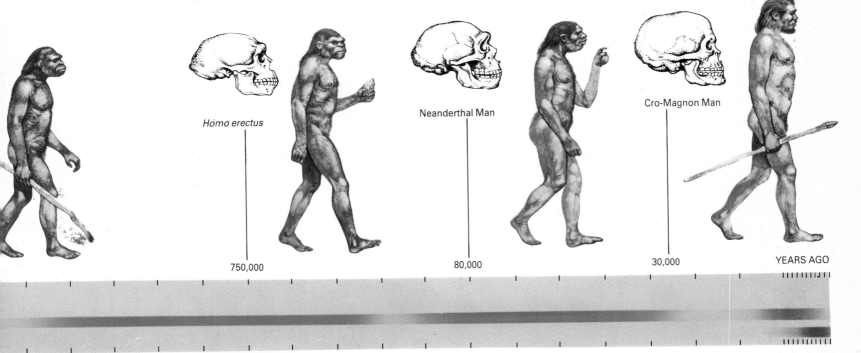

Homo erectus

Neanderthal Man

Cro-Magnon Man

750,000

80,000

30,000

YEARS AGO

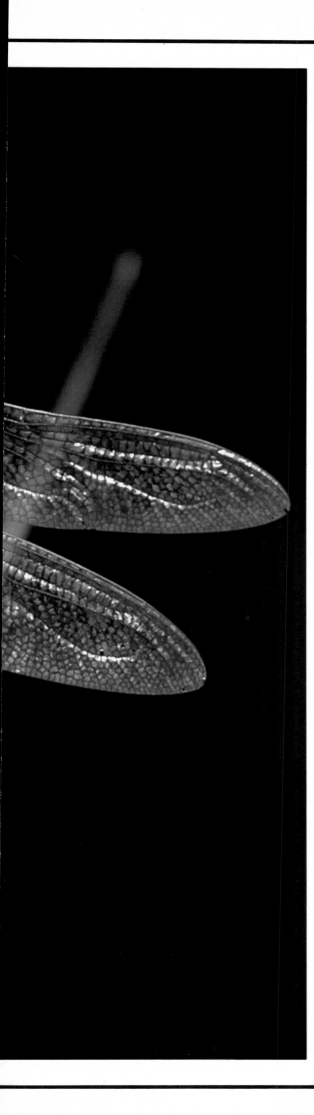

Chapter 3
Survivors *and* *Specialists*

In evolution, as in business life, whether you are a success or a failure depends partly on your abilities, partly on your luck. The marsupials of Australia were lucky to survive for so long in isolation, free from dangerous competition with more able placental mammals. The ancient mammal populations of South America were not so lucky – they were wiped out by this kind of competition.

If we regard a successful animal or plant as well designed for survival, then there are at least three good designs. First, 'safe' designs continue to last. The crocodiles, tortoises, brachiopods, ferns and conifers have all been around for a very long time. Second, flexible designs are very adaptable to changing conditions. Rats, human beings and gorse bushes are good examples – they all tend to spread widely. Third is the specialized design. Giraffes, many kinds of parasites, and a bacterium which lives in boiling hot springs, are only a few examples. In their different ways, these have all made sure of their livelihood by developing to the utmost their special abilities.

An animal's behaviour also affects its ability to survive. Some animals have evolved amazing courtship rituals to ensure they breed only with their own species. Some insects on the other hand parody other species to protect them from predators.

A successful survivor is the emperor dragonfly, a member of one of the most ancient of insect groups with a history going back to the time of the coal forests. The dragonfly's four large wings and great, multifaceted eyes aid it in its fast, accurate flight in search of prey or a mate.

Life's Best Designs

EVOLUTION OF THE HEART

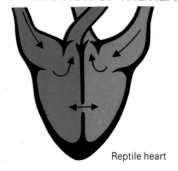
Reptile heart

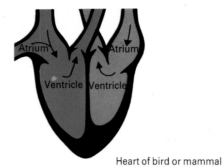
Atrium   Atrium
Ventricle Ventricle
Heart of bird or mammal

Amphibian heart

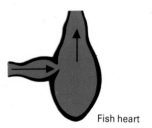
Fish heart

Above: The evolution of the vertebrate heart is shown by comparing this organ in the main groups of living backboned animals. The heart of a fish is a fairly simple, single pump, whereas that of a bird or mammal is a complex double pump. The arrows show the directions of blood flow.

We have already seen how one living group can succeed at the expense of another. The mammals evolved a general level of flexibility which the reptiles could not hope to match. Accordingly the mammals increased in numbers and varieties, while the reptiles declined.

Particular clues to the mammals' success are to be found in their better brains, and more effective reproductive system and body temperature control. These involved not only improvements to existing organs – bigger brain, hairy skin – but also to the invention of new uses for old organs – the uterus from part of the egg-laying system and the mammary glands from sweat glands. New and improved organs are often vivid indicators of evolutionary progress. A further example already mentioned is the evolution of vascular organs – transport tubes – which enabled plants to colonize the land. Nature offers many examples, a few of which we can look at briefly.

Organ Evolution
Some new organs evolved without leaving many clues as to their origins. One such is the backbone, or rather, the large nerve cord that lies inside it. A surprising fact here is that all the most highly advanced invertebrate animals, such as insects, lobsters and squids, have their main nerve cord on the underside of their bodies, that is, on the opposite side to the backbone of vertebrates. This means that no such advanced invertebrate is a very likely candidate as the original ancestor of backboned animals, because far too much reorganization of the body would have been involved in turning the contents of the body upside down. Who, then, are our remote invertebrate ancestors? The group now favoured (see pages 44–45 for the rather complicated reasons) is in many ways one of the least apparently likely. The ECHINODERMS, including the starfishes, sea cucumbers and sea lilies, not only lack a backbone but even a main nerve cord! It would seem that nature invented these two organs afresh, to make the vertebrates.

The origins of many other animal organs are, however, much less difficult to find. Some organs have clearly evolved from already existing organs that served a quite different purpose. The jaws of backboned animals originated in this way from the gill bars of early jawless fishes. The most frontal of these bony gill stiffeners swung down and forward, and then enlarged, to make the hinged lower jaw of the first jawed fishes.

Among higher plants an example of this kind is the flower, an organ of reproduction which almost certainly evolved from a leaf, an organ of PHOTOSYNTHESIS. Exactly how this happened is, however, far less clear than the evolution of the vertebrate jaw.

Sometimes, the way in which an organ has evolved is very clear indeed because we can examine it at various stages of development in different living groups. This is the case with the vertebrate heart, which is two-chambered in fishes, three-chambered in amphibians and four-chambered in reptiles, birds and mammals. The diagrams show this progress in design together with a few other evolutionary heart improvements.

Perhaps the finest candidates for the title of life's best designs are those in which

Left: A living example of a jawless fish – a river lamprey. Its several, clearly visible gills are supported internally by stiff skeletal bars lying between the gill openings. From the most forwardly placed of such gill bars evolved the jaws of backboned animals. This happened among Devonian fishes, as shown below.

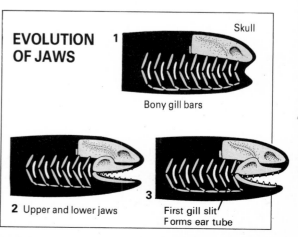
EVOLUTION OF JAWS
1 Skull
Bony gill bars
2 Upper and lower jaws
3 First gill slit Forms ear tube

nature has repeated herself, sometimes several times over. This is particularly noticeable with animals that are more or less unrelated but that have come to resemble one another closely. A more scientific way of putting this is to say that, among animals with similar lifestyles, natural selection favours a resemblance. This is known as CONVERGENT EVOLUTION.

Convergent Evolution

Mammals, which lead more varied lives than other land vertebrates, are particularly rich in startling examples of convergent evolution. But to take first a rather unlikely case, we can say that the horse is a highly remarkable kind of mammal, particularly with regard to its single-toed foot. Even so, another plains animal, belonging to a now totally extinct South American group, the litopterns, paralleled the horse in almost every respect, including the single toe.

Mole-like mammals include the familiar garden mole (a member of the insectivore group), several kinds of tunnelling rodents known as mole rats, and the completely unrelated marsupial mole of Australia. In this example, evolutionary convergence extends even beyond the backboned animals. The mole crickets are a group of burrowing insects having powerful, shovel-like front legs, a velvety coat and a cylindrical body, closely resembling miniature moles.

A better-known resemblance between animals having widely separated ancestry is that between whales and fishes. To gain their present shape, whales have descended, by a remarkable series of adaptations, from CREODONTS, extinct four-footed land carnivores that looked rather like giant weasels. Seals, sealions and walruses have also descended from the ancient creodonts but their adaptations to a marine life have been less complete than those of the whales.

Of course, convergent evolution is by no means confined to mammals but has taken place throughout the animal and plant kingdoms. To take an example from among the birds, we can consider those acrobatic insect-chasers of summer skies, the swallows, martins and swifts. Swallows and martins are first cousins but neither is closely related to the swifts, even though all three are similarly fast-flying, narrow-winged insect-eaters. The swifts' own cousins are to be found in tropical forests as the tiny, brilliant humming birds.

Examples of convergence among plants perhaps seem less exciting, except for those with some knowledge of botany. However, one that certainly deserves mention here is *Gingko biloba*, better known as the Maidenhair tree. To a casual stroller in a botanical garden, the Maidenhair might look very like a flowering broad-leaved tree. A second, closer look would show that its broad leaves have a rather peculiar shape. In fact, the Maidenhair tree is a LIVING FOSSIL, far more ancient than any flowering

An example of convergent evolution among unrelated flowering plants. The large cactus, above, and the tree spurge, left, are cleverly and very similarly adapted to a life in dry regions.

plant and not even closely related to its fellow conifers.

From the great selection that nature offers, a final example of convergent evolution can be taken not from a whole creature, but from a single animal organ, the eye.

Squids, octopuses and cuttlefishes are active sea creatures that hunt their prey at speed with the help of their well-developed eyes. These eyes are constructed very similarly to our own and those of other vertebrates, with a single, movable lens and a complex retina. Yet these molluscs are about as distantly related to vertebrates as it is possible to be. The nearest ancestor shared by the two groups would be some ancient type of worm – possibly eyeless!

An example of convergent evolution among similar, but unrelated, tunnelling mammals. Below: A common garden mole, which is an insectivore. Left: A mole rat, which is a rodent.

Nature's Conservatives

A tuatara basks on Stephens Island, its New Zealand home. Although superficially like a lizard, it is really a far more ancient type of reptile, which has remained virtually unchanged since long before the dinosaurs.

The tortoises and turtles mentioned earlier are the oldest of living reptiles. The tuatara of New Zealand is almost as old. Although superficially lizard-like, it is really far more ancient than any lizard, and is the only land animal to retain a working PINEAL EYE – a third eye opening on the roof of its skull.

Such creatures as the tuatara well deserve the name living fossil because they are the last survivors of their groups, soldiering on alone through the ages. Other examples we have already encountered are the coelacanth, last survivor of the lobefin ancestors of land animals, and the maidenhair tree. Among trees, a good example is the cycad, a stumpy, palm-like cone-bearer, growing in hot climates. It was much more numerous and widespread in the far-off days of the coal swamps.

The Importance of a Good Niche

We can say that such living fossils are lucky still to be around when so many of their near relatives have become extinct. But what, in evolutionary terms, does 'lucky' mean?

An answer to this question can often be obtained by looking at the lifestyle of a particular organism. Like people, individual animals, plants and microbes have particular trades and professions. Carnivore, or meat-eater, is one great animal profession. There are various branches of this profession: marine carnivore, mud-dwelling carnivore, aerial carnivore, and so on. Other great natural professions include herbivore, parasite, SAPROPHYTE and photosynthesizer. Any of these natural professions or their various branches is what is called an ENVIRONMENTAL NICHE – what an organism does.

Also like people, all other organisms have a home address, or, in biological terms, a HABITAT. A rabbit's habitat is *earth burrow and meadow*; a gannet's *cliff and sea-sky*; an amoeba's *pond mud*.

A living fossil can be thought of as having a secure profession. That is, its environmental niche will be a stable, long-lasting one. Also, it is likely to have a good address – its habitat is a safe and secure one. The tuatara, for example, is one of the few carnivores (niche) on its island home (habitat) off the New Zealand coast.

Nature's Methuselahs

To find nature's oldest inhabitants of all, it is necessary to look in places where the environment is stable and competition is low, so that an organism has the chance to 'capture the local market'. One such place is the sea floor, vast stretches of which, untouched as yet even by man the polluter, house a huge number of small creatures, some with very long pedigrees.

The world record for the oldest living animal GENUS is, in fact, held by a marine mud-dweller named *Lingula*, which has remained more or less unchanged in its muddy burrow for no less than 500 million years. *Lingula* belongs to the two-shelled marine animals called the brachiopods, long ago a great group but now reduced to a few hundred species.

Even more ancient groups are those of simpler one-celled or few-celled organisms such as the BLUEGREEN ALGAE and the bacteria. Photosynthetic bacteria may be the oldest of all. They live in airless conditions near the surface of mud, using the energy of sunlight to make their own food. This lifestyle predates even the Earth's oxygen atmosphere, 2000 million years ago.

Above: The maidenhair tree, Latin name *Gingko biloba*, is a living fossil from China. The sole remaining species of its group, it is distantly related to such different types of tree as the pines and the cycads.

Below: The horseshoe crab or king crab is not, in fact, a crab at all, but an ancient relative of spiders and scorpions.

Below: The solenodon of Cuba and Haiti is just what it looks like, a survivor of a very ancient stock of mammals. Fossils of these clumsy, long-nosed insectivores date from as long ago as 30 million years.

Below right: The most conservative animal genus of all, *Lingula*, at home in its muddy burrow, has a fossil history extending back no less than 500 million years. It is a brachiopod or lamp shell.

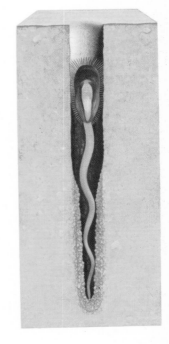

Nature's Specialists

Right: A strange plant with a strange name, *Welwitschia* **lives only in the desert areas of South-west Africa. Its two giant leaves continue to grow for a hundred years from their great, flat, woody base, and are gradually worn away at the tips by the desert sands.** *Welwitschia* **is classified by botanists between the conifers and the flowering plants.**

Above: A sidewinding viper advances steadily across African desert sands. This curious method of locomotion is, in fact, an excellent adaptation for a life in hot deserts. It enables the snake to progress easily through loose sand, and because the snake's body makes contact with the hot sand at only two points, it does not become overheated.

Below: Blandford's jerboa, a nocturnal desert rodent with long, kangaroo-like jumping legs. Jerboas are remarkably well adapted for conserving water in their bodies and have been known to go without drinking for several years.

Below: Arabian (one-humped) camels in the Libyan desert. Camels are a walking compendium of desert adaptations. Their long bodies and spindly legs are shaped to lose heat; their toes are splayed, padded and webbed for walking over loose sand; their nostrils can be shut tight to keep out sand, and their large eyes are protected against blown sand by long eyelashes. The hump, however, does not carry water – it is a fatty food reserve.

An animal or plant species will live on untouched by evolutionary change if it finds itself in a stable habitat free of competitors and well supplied with the necessities of life. The sea floor provides many such habitats because it is uniformly vast, is at a fairly even and moderate temperature, and is bathed in water carrying vital oxygen and food organisms.

But what of life in the opposite kind of environment, where harsh and extreme conditions are the rule? Waterless deserts, freezing polar seas, lightless ocean deeps, acid bogs and hot springs are all very hostile places. Nevertheless, these all harbour life, because life has a wonderful capacity for making the most of small opportunities.

Life at Extremes

Not surprisingly, populations in some of these extreme environments tend to be small or sparse. Also, individual organisms are likely to be specially adapted to meet the harsh demands of their surroundings.

Among desert animals, the large ears of desert foxes are an obvious ADAPTATION for losing heat – Arctic foxes, by contrast, have small ears. Another desert animal, the sidewinder viper, adapts itself for progress through loose desert sands by special and peculiar body movements. Desert animals in general show protective adaptations of behaviour, the most obvious of which is keeping out of the sun by burrowing and coming out to feed only in the cooler night.

Most famous of desert plants are, of course, the cacti, in which the green stem has swollen to store and conserve water, while the leaves have become mere spines,

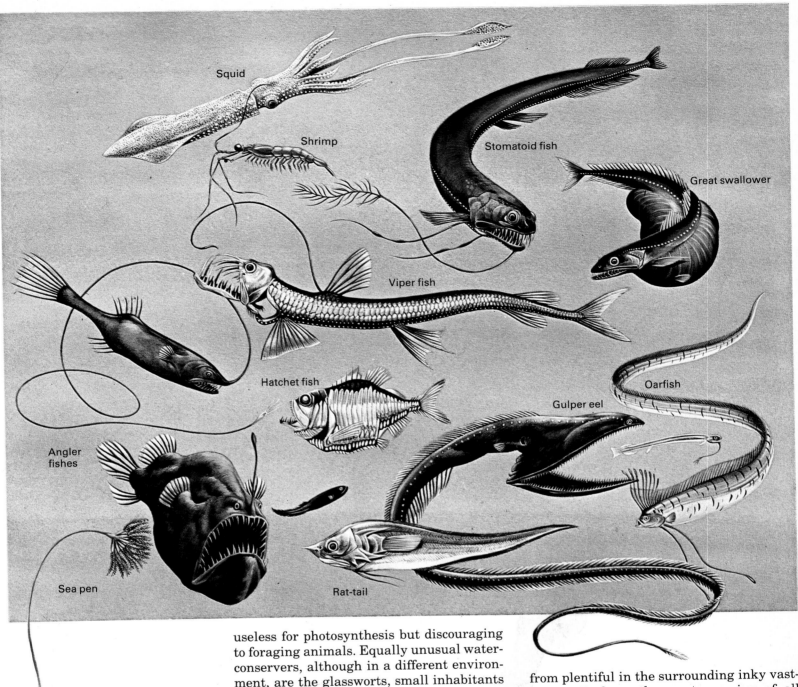

Squid

Shrimp

Stomatoid fish

Great swallower

Viper fish

Angler fishes

Hatchet fish

Oarfish

Gulper eel

Sea pen

Rat-tail

Above: Strange creatures of the ocean depths. The scene drawn is a crowded one, but in reality life is very sparsely distributed two kilometres or a mile or more down. This helps to explain many of the more bizarre adaptations of the deep sea animals. The great gaping mouths and enormously distensible stomachs of some deep-sea fishes reflect the scarcity of their prey – a meal has to last a long time! Most deep-sea fishes also have lightweight bodies with flimsy skeletons which need little effort to propel them through the water. Many remain motionless for long periods, fishing for prey with luminous lures. Others use their luminous organs to attract a possible mate, or to deceive a predator as to their true body outline.

useless for photosynthesis but discouraging to foraging animals. Equally unusual water-conservers, although in a different environment, are the glassworts, small inhabitants of salt marshes. These get their name from their glassy, swollen stems, which bear tiny, scale-like leaves. Although they live surrounded by water, this is so toxic with salt that glassworts have as great a need to retain water as cacti.

Polar seas are as coldly unfriendly as tropical deserts are uncomfortably hot. Fishes that live in them must withstand temperatures down to −2°C (28·4°F), where the slightest further temperature drop would freeze them solid. Some polar fishes show very striking adaptations to their severe environment. They have large gills for taking in a good supply of oxygen, but pallid, ghostly bodies lacking red blood cells. In their cold blood, oxygen dissolves readily without the need for the red pigment HAEMOGLOBIN.

Even more bizarre are many deep sea fishes fitted out with brilliantly glowing lures and rows of luminous 'portholes', which serve such purposes as attracting victims and mates, both of which are far

from plentiful in the surrounding inky vastnesses. Perhaps the most amazing of all these creatures of the middle deep are the gulper eels, with jaws half the weight of their bodies, and stomachs that distend like elastic bags to hold and digest prey larger than themselves.

In acid waters, such as those of marshes and bogs, lack of the element nitrogen, vital for proteins, discourages the growth of most forms of life. Certain flowering plants have overcome this difficulty by capturing their own nitrogen, in the form of insects and other small creatures, which they then digest, sometimes with the aid of special enzyme-secreting glands. The sundew, Venus flytrap and bladderwort are examples of these carnivorous plants.

There are certain microscopic algae and bacteria which live in hot springs at temperatures as high as 80°C (176°F). This lifestyle requires nothing less than a completely special set of enzymes. Those of any other creature would be inactivated by the heat – the creature would boil alive.

Neoteny, or Growing Up Young

Above: Ostriches, the largest of living birds, have a number of chick-like features, including downy feathers.

When a tadpole changes into a frog, its body loses its tail and gills and instead sprouts legs and lungs. This radical alteration, or metamorphosis, is controlled by the thyroid gland. If an extract of thyroid gland (a cow's will do) is added to water containing young tadpoles, they will metamorphose early into miniature frogs or froglets. If, in a tricky operation, a tadpole's thyroid gland is removed, then the tadpole will not metamor-

phose into a frog at all but will grow up to be a giant tadpole.

In some of the frog's far-flung relatives, this permanently juvenile state occurs naturally. The axolotl is a giant tadpole that usually stays that way but can be made to change into a tiger salamander by the administration of thyroid extract. The mudpuppy is another salamander tadpole, but one that cannot metamorphose.

Both the axolotl and the mudpuppy, although juvenile in form, can lay eggs in the adult manner, which then develop into further generations of grown-up tadpoles. This growing-up-young is known as NEOTENY. Throughout the ages, it has happened widely in nature, and is responsible for a number of important evolutionary developments, at least two of which strongly affect ourselves.

Man, Ape and Ostrich

The more recent of these effects concerns our descent from ape-like ancestors. If we compare the shape of a human skull with that of our nearest ape relative, the chimpanzee, it obviously looks more like the skull of a baby chimp than that of an adult chimp. This does not mean that we are descended from baby chimps, but that the human line probably

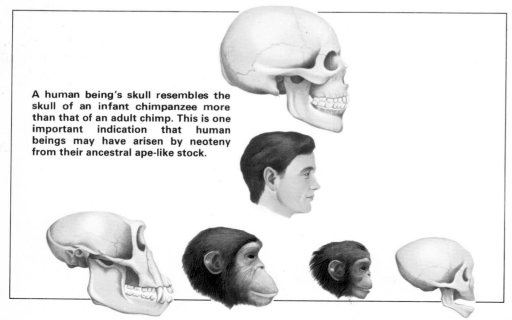

A human being's skull resembles the skull of an infant chimpanzee more than that of an adult chimp. This is one important indication that human beings may have arisen by neoteny from their ancestral ape-like stock.

arose by neoteny from some ancestor who was also the ancestor of the chimp (and of the gorilla too).

Biologists even have a shrewd idea of how this could have happened. In the higher primates sexual development is strongly influenced by the adrenal glands. Overactivity of these glands in a young boy can cause him to become sexually mature well before the normal age of puberty. This could have happened in our ape-like ancestor, helping to give rise to a new, more human-like variety.

Another group of animals which clearly arose by neoteny are those great flightless birds the ostrich, emu, cassowary and rhea, together with the smaller kiwi of New Zealand, itself a close relative of the recently extinct giant moas. Although it is considerably the largest of living birds, the ostrich has the fluffy plumage of a chick. The same applies, rather less obviously, to the emu, cassowary, rhea and kiwi. Actually, despite their resemblances, few of these birds are closely related, so that neoteny would have occurred in their ancestry several times.

Vertebrate Ancestors

It seems probable that neoteny was responsible for the first appearance of the backboned animals, the great group to which we and all other higher animals belong. This ancestry is, however, less easy to trace than that of the ape/human stock.

Vertebrates are really part of a slightly larger group called the CHORDATES, which also contains some members which never develop backbones at all. However, like

Above: The axolotl is a giant tadpole, which usually does not metamorphose into an adult salamander, but reproduces while still in the juvenile gilled stage. (This one is an albino, the pigmented varieties being dark brown or black.)

vertebrate embryos, they do develop a tubular pre-backbone called the notochord.

Among these non-vertebrate chordates are the sea squirts and the acorn worms, marine animals that look very little like any backboned animal. The LARVA of the sea squirts, however, is a tadpole-like creature having a well-defined notochord – which gets lost in the adult. From such a tadpole-like larva, the first backboned animal could have arisen by neoteny.

The adult acorn worm does have a short, notochord-like structure. Now, *its* larva looks nothing like a tadpole, but greatly resembles the larva of the echinoderms or spiny-skinned invertebrates. These facts, together with some more complicated biochemical evidence, lead many biologists to identify the original vertebrate ancestor with that of such unlikely modern creatures as starfishes and sea cucumbers.

The possible origin of backboned animals by neoteny. Echinoderms and acorn worms look very unalike, but are probably related because their tiny larvae closely resemble each other. The acorn worm has a small internal structure which resembles the notochord of embryonic backboned animals. A notochord is more prominent in the small, rather fish-like lancelet, and in the tadpole-like larva of the sea squirt. From such larvae could have arisen the jawless fishes, earliest of the vertebrates.

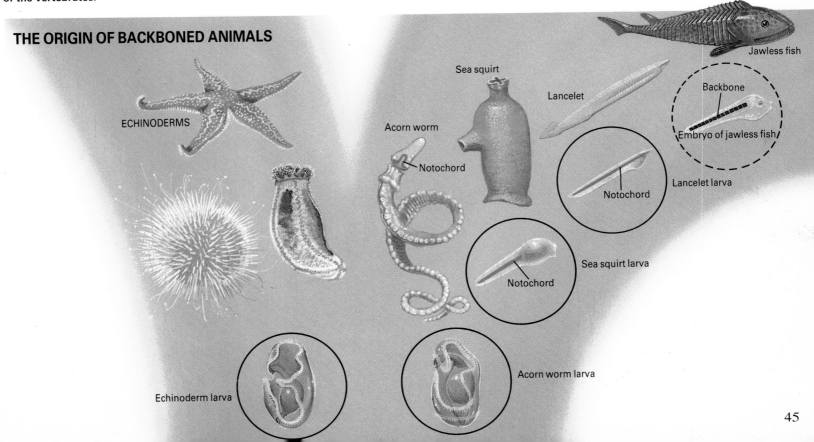

THE ORIGIN OF BACKBONED ANIMALS

ECHINODERMS

Acorn worm

Notochord

Sea squirt

Lancelet

Jawless fish

Backbone

Embryo of jawless fish

Notochord

Lancelet larva

Notochord

Sea squirt larva

Acorn worm larva

Echinoderm larva

Partners and Rivals

The most obvious kind of partnership in nature is that between two mating individuals. In this partnership, the sexes are sometimes very similar in appearance – for example, the Canada goose and gander – and sometimes very distinct – the mallard duck and drake. Any such obvious difference between sexual partners is called a sexual dimorphism. Among higher animals such as birds and mammals, it is the male that usually has the display features – the brighter colours of the mallard drake, the larger antlers of the stag, the greater bulk of the bull, are all good examples.

Charles Darwin believed that these male display features were important for a special type of selection, which he named sexual selection. An obvious instance of sexual selection would be that larger stags with bigger antlers have greater success and mate with more hinds to produce a more numerous progeny.

Left: The cock and hen red-capped robin are a clear instance of sexual dimorphism.

Below: Two mountain bighorn sheep establish their rank in the herd by butting each other. One will almost certainly emerge from the contest as dominant to the other, although most probably neither will have been hurt at all seriously.

Many evolutionists today would still agree on the importance of sexual selection. It is, after all, part of natural selection but with another animal doing the selecting instead of cold weather or lack of food.

Social Behaviour

Sexual selection is really just one aspect of social behaviour – the way in which animals behave with one another. At one time biologists were puzzled by the evolution of many types of social behaviour. Why should two animals, such as stags, have a ritual fight in which the winner does not really hurt the loser? For if the winner killed the loser he would have one less rival to worry about.

Some biologists said that this type of social behaviour evolved by group selection for the good of the species; if stags fought to kill they might both be seriously wounded and die. Therefore rituals evolved for the good of the species. Yet any stag that cheated (by fighting to kill) would become very successful. His rivals would not try to kill him but he would kill them and mate with all the hinds. He would father many sons, and soon all stags would be killers again.

This is a common fault in group selection explanations of social behaviour. The system is open to exploitation by cheats and soon breaks down.

Another common result of social behaviour is a DOMINANCE hierarchy, or pecking order. Animals high in the order take precedence over others. The dominant female in a wolf pack, for example, is the only female in the pack who breeds. The other wolves help her to raise the cubs. Why should subordinate wolves stay in the pack but not breed? Again there is no need to say that it is for the good of the pack. It is possible to think of good selfish reasons for this ALTRUISTIC BEHAVIOUR.

The most important reason is probably that the females in the pack are related. When they help the dominant female they are helping their sister, and the cubs are relatives too. The subordinates have genes in common with the cubs (although not as many as with their own cubs) and the relationship is close enough to make it worthwhile helping the dominant female to rear her cubs. This is called KIN SELECTION.

Among the most complex and remarkable of all animal societies are colonies of social insects such as ants, wasps, bees and termites. Some colonies can harbour not only females, males and juveniles, but also various kinds of sterile adult workers and soldiers, parasitic 'lodgers', captured slave workers and insects milked for their sweet secretions. The behaviour of all these inhabitants, in all its complexity, affects the success or failure of the COLONY – but the death or survival of individual members (except the queen) counts hardly at all.

Below: These timber wolves may look alike, but in fact each wolf has its particular social level, or status. A dominant wolf will usually elicit submissive behaviour from a wolf of lower rank. Because of this accepted order of rank, few really serious fights break out between members of the group.

Below: Termites are social insects which, even more than honey bees (*not* near relations), show a remarkable polymorphism, or range of forms. In many ways, a colony of social insects behaves as a single living organism in which the different types of individuals resemble specialized groups of cells. The queen produces eggs and is fed and looked after by the workers. The workers also clean and repair the nest and forage for food. Soldier termites escort workers and defend the nest. Small soldiers also guide and control the ceaseless activity inside the nest.

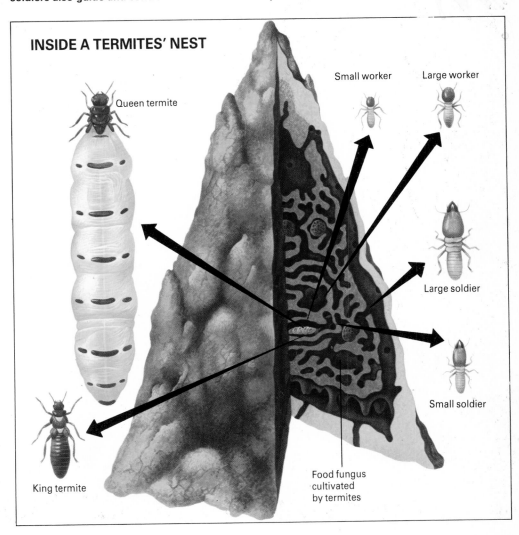

INSIDE A TERMITES' NEST

Queen termite

Small worker

Large worker

Large soldier

Small soldier

King termite

Food fungus cultivated by termites

Isolation and Competition

Evolutionary change has often been brought about by geographical isolation. The first finches to land on the Galápagos Islands probably looked and behaved like average finches. In their new home, they found many more ecological niches open to them, which they were able to fill, so that when Darwin got to the islands he found finches filling the roles of warblers and woodpeckers.

On a very much larger scale, the early mammals radiated to fill the ecological niches left behind by the disappearing reptiles. In North America, these niches were largely taken up by placental mammals of kinds familiar to us. In South America, which was at that time isolated from North America by a sea-gap at Panama, a quite different, though even more diverse, population arose. This was composed of old-fashioned marsupials, together with placental mammals quite unrelated to modern types yet often bearing a strange resemblance to them. Because the placentals were all herbivores, the marsupials were able to survive along with them.

One animal already mentioned, a member of the litopterns, looked very like a horse, even down to the single toe. Another closely resembled a llama, except that it had an elephant-like trunk. Yet another was rhino-like in size and general appearance, although its nearest relatives included small rodent-like mammals. These are only a few members of a richly varied and unique mammal population which suffered a disastrous decline when the Panama bridge was formed.

The more modern North American mammals – among them the horse – poured across the land bridge into South America, and a few million years later, nearly all the marsupials, and most of the strange South American placentals, had disappeared. This extreme example of competition and extinction among mammals was unmatched until the appearance of mankind.

Biological Islands

Geographical separation, whether by uncrossable distances, mountain chains or sea-gaps, is only one reason for biological isolation. Species, even when closely related, often live quite separate lives although they inhabit the same geographical area. These biological islands are the result of several isolating mechanisms all of which may operate at the same time.

Ecological isolation can occur when nearby relatives occupy different habitats. For example, two mammal species or varieties

Some extinct South American mammals (and a bird) of the Pliocene epoch. They thrived in Patagonia and the lush forests and grasslands of South America until the late Pliocene when they faced disastrous competition from the North American mammals which had come over the recently formed land bridge. These extinct mammals showed remarkable similarities to many modern mammals, to which they are not closely related.

Macrauchenia looked like a llama but may have been amphibious

Megatherium was a giant sloth

Diadiaphorus resembled an early horse

Glyptodon was a giant armadillo

may not interbreed because they hunt different prey and so only rarely come into contact with one another. More examples of ecological isolation are provided, again, by Darwin's finches, which although very closely interrelated, are separated into types which fly, feed and perch at higher or lower levels in bushes and trees.

Reproductive isolation happens between species which may be obviously closely related, yet which differ genetically to an extent that makes them incompatible. A good example here is the little fruit fly *Drosophila*, which has several species, all very alike to the layman, yet different in as many as 40% of their GENES.

Seasonal isolation occurs when closely related creatures have different breeding times. A remarkable example is that of certain cicadas, tree insects famous for their loud, trilling song, but which spend most of their long lives as underground larvae. In North America the 13-year cicada and the 17-year cicada are both named after the length of their larval lives. They do not interbreed because the years of their emergence rarely coincide.

The evolutionary significance of such examples is that the organisms concerned, isolated on their biological islands, seldom exchange genes with one another and so become more different over time.

Above right: Not all the South American mammals were extinguished by their North American competitors. This furry armadillo, now living in North America, is a much smaller relative of the extinct *Glyptodon*.

Right: These llamas in Peru are descendants of the incoming northern mammals who took over from the litopterns, such as *Macrauchenia* and *Diadiaphorus*, and other herbivores.

Thilacosmilus was a marsupial sabretooth

Toxodon resembled a hippo but was more nearly a giant guinea pig

Diatryma, a giant flesh-eating bird, and *Astrapotherium*, a large mammal, resembled no modern animals

Survival Strategy

Right: The bee orchid has evolved a shape, colour and pattern that mimics the body of a female bee, deceiving male bees into trying to copulate with it. In this way pollen gets transferred by the bees from flower to flower.

Below: A plaice lies camouflaged on its habitat, the sea bed. It can change its colour pattern to match particular backgrounds.

Bottom: A yellow-bellied mountain toad bears a bright yellow-and-blue warning coloration, which tells its enemies that it tastes very unpleasant.

In a world whose motto is 'eat or be eaten' both predators and prey can gain advantages through changes brought about by natural selection. One of the most important ways in which this can happen is by the evolution of special colours and patterns.

Simple examples are provided by camouflage or CRYPTIC COLORATION. The moth whose colour-pattern best matches that of the tree trunk on which it rests, is least likely to get picked off by birds. And the more a mantis comes to resemble a green stick, the more likely it is that unwary prey will come within striking distance of this predatory insect's forelegs.

Distasteful Advertising

Many insects are avoided by birds and other predators because they either taste nasty or are poisonous, or have a sting or venomous bite. Young birds have to learn the penalty for eating such unpalatable insects, but the insects themselves have helped by evolving bright, highly visible warning patterns in red, black, white and yellow.

Other insects living in their vicinity may also show this WARNING COLORATION, even though they are really quite harmless and palatable. This protective MIMICRY extends also to shape – hoverflies, for example, are not only banded black and yellow, but also have a rather wasp-like body shape.

But mimicry is only an advantage to tasty insects when there are fewer of them than the distasteful insects they mimic. Otherwise, birds might come to associate the bright, mimicked colours with tastiness! In fact, insect mimics often 'choose' to mimic not one but several distasteful species. In this way, their own numbers can increase while they still enjoy protection.

Yet other insects mimic unattractive objects such as bird droppings, or deter predators by flashing at them brightly coloured spots which are mistaken for the eyes of larger animals.

Cuckoos and Other Parasites

The European cuckoo, a well-known parasite of other birds, also uses the strategy of mimicry. It does not itself resemble its host birds, but lays eggs which cleverly mimic those of the hosts, which for this reason seldom remove the fatal object from their nest.

Parasitism itself is a life-strategy, or rather a whole series of strategies. Most parasites, unlike the cuckoo, are much smaller than their hosts, and pass from host to host by the processes we know as infections or infestations. Parasites such as blood-sucking ticks, intestinal worms and disease-causing bacteria may seem to us unpleasant products of nature. Yet even they can be seen to play a useful role in the natural control of animal numbers. A population explosion among a host species may threaten its entire habitat with destruction, but this threat is usually countered by the more rapid spread of parasites through the overcrowded population. This in turn weeds out weaker individuals and also tends to reduce fertility generally. When host numbers drop, epidemics also tend to die down and the reduced host population regains its health and vigour.

Right: Parasitism is a very widespread mode of life. This roach suffered from a very large internal parasite, the tapeworm *Ligula*, which has been removed from the fish's body for inspection.

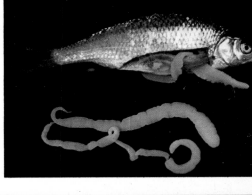

Below: Symbiosis is an intimate association between different species. This species of the simple animal *Hydra* is green because of the presence in its body of many *Zoochlorellae*, symbiotic single-cell algae.

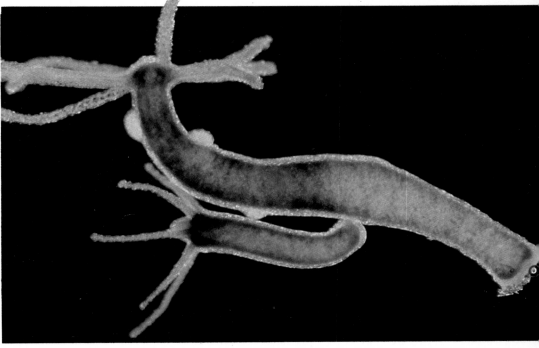

Chapter *4*
What Causes
Variety?

The variety of life is the most important aspect of evolutionary progress. But what exactly causes this variety? In other words, what has produced the immense numbers of different animals (more than a million living species), plants (at least half a million species), and microbes (at least as many again)? Part of the answer to this question is, of course, natural selection. But selection, by its very name, is really a force for *reducing* variety. Of the huge numbers of varieties offered it by nature, natural selection weeds out those least likely to survive. The forces that actually *produce* variety act inside the living cell, particularly in reproductive cells such as eggs and sperm, and eggs and pollen, which come together in the act of fertilization. This is the same as saying that sex produces variety. Inside any living cell, all the genetic information which is needed for producing variety is chemically coded in the genes, the units of heredity which parents pass on to their offspring.

A colourful display of sweet peas. Gregor Mendel, with his breeding experiments using pea plants, answered the first great question concerning heredity – in what ways are characteristics of parents distributed among their offspring?

Mendel Explains Heredity

If asked the question 'What is it in your body that causes you to be different from any other person?' you would probably answer 'My genes'.

Darwin, however, knew nothing of genes. In his day, the sciences of BIOCHEMISTRY and MOLECULAR BIOLOGY, which are needed to explain what a gene is, had not even been invented. Darwin's own ideas on heredity – the way we inherit our parents' own characteristics – were similar to those of Lamarck a generation previously. Both men felt sure that new characteristics, acquired during a lifetime, could somehow be passed on to the next generation. Neither had a convincing explanation of just how this could happen, so that the idea of inheritance of acquired characteristics remained vague.

Below: Pure-bred tall and short plants each have two identical factors for height in their body cells. But their sex cells receive only one of these factors. Progeny receive one factor from each parent.

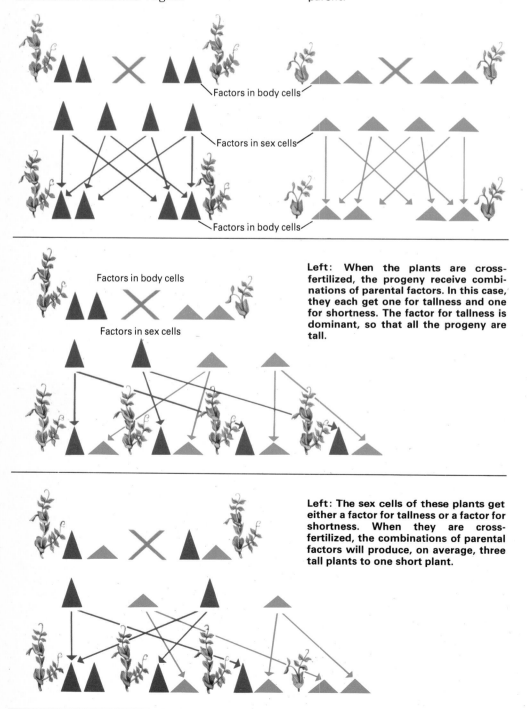

Left: When the plants are cross-fertilized, the progeny receive combinations of parental factors. In this case, they each get one for tallness and one for shortness. The factor for tallness is dominant, so that all the progeny are tall.

Left: The sex cells of these plants get either a factor for tallness or a factor for shortness. When they are cross-fertilized, the combinations of parental factors will produce, on average, three tall plants to one short plant.

Gregor Mendel and his Peas

In 1859 Darwin published *The Origin of Species*, explaining the importance to evolution of natural selection, and became world famous. In 1866, only seven years later, a Moravian monk named Gregor MENDEL published a much shorter scientific paper explaining the laws of heredity, and was ignored even by the small scientific establishment of his own country.

Mendel's work was rediscovered and given its due recognition only at the turn of the 20th century. It was then seen to be of revolutionary importance because it explained both the general way in which parents transmit their characteristics, and also the frequency with which these characteristics appear among their offspring.

In the peace of his monastery garden, Mendel bred pea plants, crossing one with the other by artificial pollination. Each parent plant had a number of well-defined characteristics such as tallness and shortness, and Mendel looked for the same features in the offspring that grew from his crosses.

He had noticed that parental features such as these tended to appear among the offspring in a regular, rather than a random, fashion. This suggested to him that something specific was being handed on which caused a particular feature to appear. We should call this something a gene, but Mendel, like his contemporary Darwin, knew nothing of genes. He called the handed-on something a hereditary factor.

Obviously, since such factors came from both parents, they were present in the pollen and egg cells, since these were the only parts of the parents to come into contact during pollination.

BLUE EYES OR BROWN?

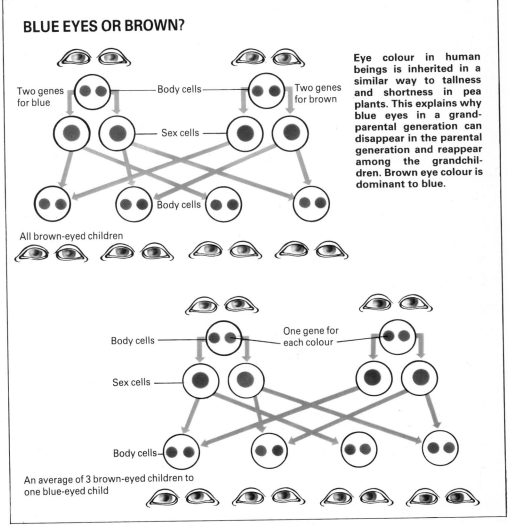

Two genes for blue — Body cells — Two genes for brown

Sex cells

Body cells

All brown-eyed children

Eye colour in human beings is inherited in a similar way to tallness and shortness in pea plants. This explains why blue eyes in a grand-parental generation can disappear in the parental generation and reappear among the grandchildren. Brown eye colour is dominant to blue.

Body cells — One gene for each colour

Sex cells

Body cells

An average of 3 brown-eyed children to one blue-eyed child

Mendel's next discovery was an unexpectedly exciting one. His PURE-BRED short plants, when crossed with one another, of course produced more short plants. Similarly, his pure-bred tall plants had only tall progeny. But when he crossed pure-bred shorts with pure-bred talls, *all* of the progeny were talls. Moreover, when these tall progeny were crossed with one another, their offspring, the 'grandchildren', averaged one short to three talls.

From these remarkable results, Mendel derived his first law of heredity. This states that hereditary factors are carried individually by a parent's sex cells, and that in the fertilized egg, each factor can combine with any other similar factor from the other parent. The diagram on the left illustrates this law in the case of the tall and short pea plants. It also shows the inequality that can exist between a pair of factors. If a plant has one factor for tallness and one for shortness, then it is always tall and never short. The factor for tallness is said to be DOMINANT, and that for shortness is said to be RECESSIVE.

Mendel worked only with pea plants, but his results, and the laws he derived from them, are completely general and apply equally well to all other breeding pairs of plants or animals. This explains their revolutionary importance. Mendel's second law of heredity concerns the inheritance of pairs of associated factors, such as the colour and texture of the seeds of his pea plants. It is illustrated in the diagram on the right.

Below: Mendel's second law of heredity deals with the inheritance of two or more characteristics at the same time. By recording such characteristics as the colour and shape of the peas produced by his plants, Mendel was able to show that the factor for any one of a pair of characteristics (yellow, green) can go into a sex cell with that for any one of another pair (smooth, wrinkled). The combinations of these factors in the peas is best expressed in a grid, as shown. Notice that yellow is dominant to green, and smooth to wrinkled.

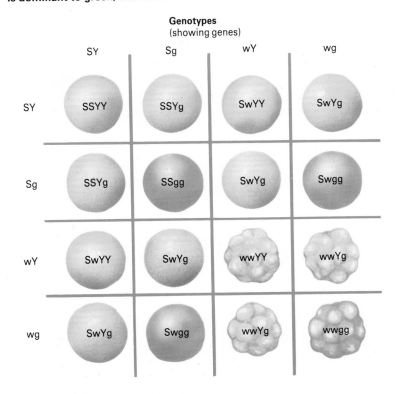

Genotypes
(showing genes)

	SY	Sg	wY	wg
SY	SSYY	SSYg	SwYY	SwYg
Sg	SSYg	SSgg	SwYg	Swgg
wY	SwYY	SwYg	wwYY	wwYg
wg	SwYg	Swgg	wwYg	wwgg

Phenotypes
(showing general appearance)

Smooth (S) and Yellow (Y)

Smooth (S) and Green (g)

Wrinkled (w) and Yellow (Y)

Wrinkled (w) and Green (g)

Parents and Children

Mendel's laws describe how particular features or traits are handed on by parents to their offspring. Different offspring will inherit different combinations of features and this will tend to produce greater variety in a population.

Darwin's law of natural selection then steps in to operate on this variety, encouraging the spread of more favourable combinations of features, and eliminating very unfavourable ones. Over a long period of time, this can lead to evolutionary changes in the population.

The Persistence of Disadvantages

But from Mendel's laws, and also from our own experience, we know that over shorter periods of time, disadvantageous features can be kept within a population. Suppose, to take the example already illustrated, that shortness is a disadvantage among a pea population. It will still be kept going by the shuffling around of inherited factors over many generations. Every now and then, a pea plant will inherit two recessive factors, or genes, for shortness and so will actually become a short plant. If shortness is a very great disadvantage indeed, then such pea plants will never live long enough to set seed, and so the gene for shortness eventually becomes very rare in the population.

In fact, shortness among peas is not so very disadvantageous. But really disadvantageous recessive traits are not difficult to find, even among human beings. Albinism, the lack of pigment in eyes and skin, is a recessive trait that is particularly disadvantageous among the Negro inhabitants of hot countries, who in this way lose their natural protection against the fierce rays of the Sun. Despite this great disadvantage, Negro populations continue to produce albinos at the rate of about one in 20,000.

Above: This Turkish father and son both show the inheritance of dominant genes for at least three facial features, namely, dark hair, dark eyes and high-bridged nose. The son, however, has not inherited his father's curly hair.

Below: The groom at this wedding has inherited the dominant gene for achondroplasia, a form of dwarfism. Other members of his family also show this trait. The bride is also achondroplastic but her family otherwise shows no evidence of the trait. Therefore, her condition may have arisen as the result of a mutation in one or another of her parent's genes.

Dominant traits, corresponding to the trait of tallness in the example of the pea plants, are widespread and can also occasionally be disadvantageous. An often seen human example is achondroplasia, a type of dwarfism in which the person has abnormally short arms and legs, but a normally-sized head, trunk – and intelligence.

Since it is a dominant trait, achondroplasia will be handed on more frequently than a recessive trait. However, this is more than counterbalanced by the tendency of achondroplastics to have fewer children than normally sized people. What prevents achondroplasia, and other dominant defects, from eventually dying out altogether, is its rare, sudden appearance among normal populations as the result of a spontaneous gene change called a MUTATION.

Gene Pools

The examples already given show that hereditary factors or genes are not so much the property of particular individuals, or even of families, as of whole populations. We have seen how even harmful traits can persist in a population because their genes are carried by many more individuals than actually suffer from the traits. Also, traits can suddenly arise if one or more genes mutate.

All the genes in a population, taken together, are called a GENE POOL. If the population is a large one, then recessive traits will crop up fairly regularly, if perhaps infrequently. But if part of a larger population takes to excessive in-breeding, then its individual members can choose only from a more limited gene pool, so that recessive traits, including disadvantageous ones, have a greater chance of appearing.

Among a closed religious group in Pennsylvania, the Amish, very short people having six fingers are fairly common. In terms of genetics, the smallness of the Amish gene pool promotes the appearance of this defect.

Chromosomes and Inheritance

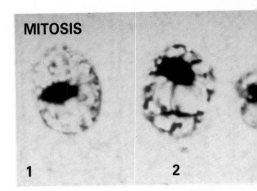

When Mendel's laws of heredity were rediscovered in 1900, sixteen years after his death, biologists began to look inside living cells for physical evidence of his hereditary factors. They had already observed, through the microscope, that when cells divide and multiply, threadlike objects appear in the cell NUCLEUS and pass in equal numbers to the 'daughter' cells produced by the division.

These threadlike objects the biologists named CHROMOSOMES, because they were parts of a living cell (soma) that could easily be stained (chroma) which made them more visible. Evidently, these chromosomes could be the carriers of Mendel's hereditary factors – which at this time one biologist renamed genes.

Gradually the evidence for this idea accumulated. Mendel's results had shown him that the cells of any individual pea plant should contain two factors for any particular characteristic, one factor having been inherited from each parent. This agreed well with the microscopists' later observations that during the division of animal and plant cells, chromosomes always appear together in the cell nucleus in matching pairs.

The idea that genes are to be found in the chromosomes was also supported strongly by the repeated observation that two or more characteristics of a plant or animal can be very strongly associated with one another, in that they are rarely or never inherited independently. This suggested that the genes for these characteristics would be linked together in some way inside the cell. Eventually, it became clear that they are

Mitosis is the process by which cells generally divide and multiply in our bodies. The photographs show a cell in various stages of mitotic division.

1 When a cell is about to divide, its chromosomes become visible in its nucleus.
2 The chromosomes separate from one another, becoming visible as long threads. The outline of the nucleus now becomes indistinct.

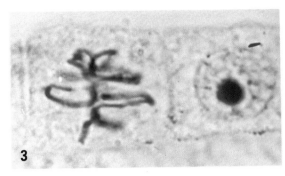
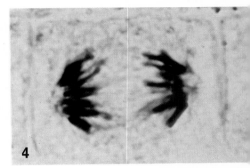

3 Each chromosome makes an exact copy of itself, and the duplicated chromosomes line up in the cell as shown.
4 The chromosomes of each duplicated pair now pull apart from one another to opposite sides of the cell.
5 A membrane begins to form inside the cell, dividing it into two daughter cells. Each daughter cell contains an exact copy of the chromosomes of the parent cell. A nucleus forms in each daughter cell to incorporate its chromosomes.

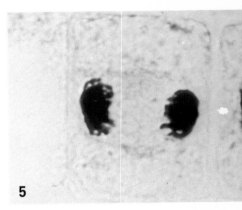

linked because they are carried on the same chromosome.

Mitosis

When a body cell divides and reproduces itself, its chromosomes duplicate and a complete set then passes to each daughter cell. This process, illustrated above, is called MITOSIS. It is the general means by which we and other animals and plants grow.

Below: A cat sometimes inherits its fur colour as a sex-linked characteristic. This ginger cat, for example, is most likely male, whereas a tortoiseshell cat is almost certainly female.

Below: The bull kudu antelope has large horns, whereas the two does have none. Both bull and does possess genes for horns, but these are expressed only in the male animal.

Meiosis

There is another type of cell division in which each daughter cell gets only half the number of chromosomes of its parent cell. This process (illustrated on the opposite page) is called MEIOSIS. It is the process by which sex cells are formed. In a human being, for example, a cell containing 46 chromosomes divides by meiosis to produce sex cells containing 23 chromosomes.

During meiosis the matching pairs of chromosomes separate from one another. Of the two copies of any parental gene, each situated on its matching chromosome, only one copy will go to any particular sex cell.

In this way, all the parental genes are distributed individually within the sex cells. Some sex cells, for example, get a dominant gene while other sex cells get a corresponding recessive gene. Also, since it is whole chromosomes that pass into the sex cells, some sperms will get an X chromosome

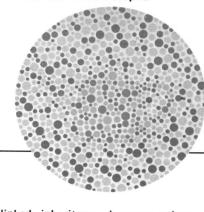

A red/green colour blindness test card. Those with normal colour vision will be able to see a teapot.

INHERITANCE OF RED/GREEN COLOUR BLINDNESS

(Men 7%, Women ½% of population)

Sex-linked inheritance happens when a gene for a particular characteristic lies on a sex chromosome. It has the peculiarity of being much commoner in one sex than in the other. Human red/green colour blindness, the example shown here, is much commoner in boys than in girls. A boy (XY) who inherits from his mother an X chromosome having the colour blindness gene, will always be colour blind. But because the gene is recessive, a girl (XX) must inherit it from both her parents if she is to be colour blind. Many defects can be inherited in this way. Some, like colour blindness, are quite harmless, but others, such as haemophilia and muscular dystrophy, are much more serious.

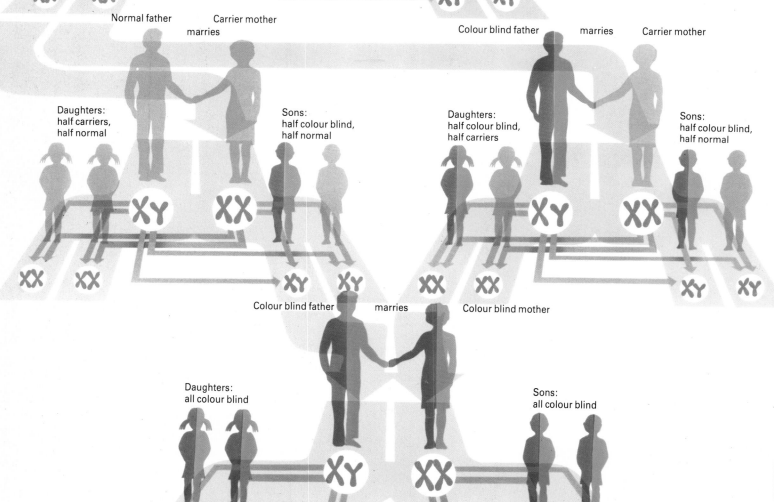

58

MEIOSIS

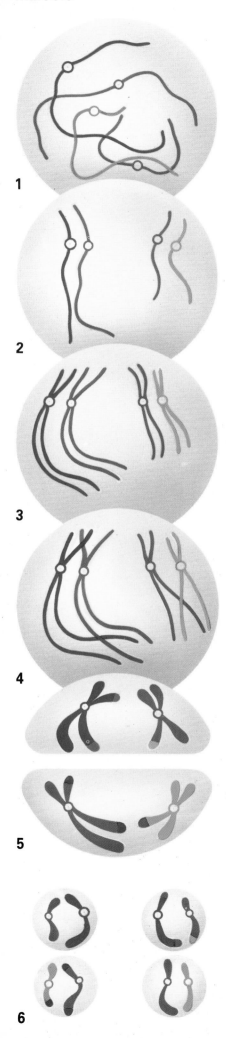

1

2

3

4

5

6

Left: Meiosis is the process of cell division by which the number of chromosomes in a cell is halved in its granddaughter cells. This happens in the production of sex cells such as ova and sperms. For simplicity, a cell having only four chromosomes is shown.
1 When the chromosomes first appear they are long, threadlike and randomly arranged.
2 They pair up and begin to shorten.
3 Each chromosome of a pair duplicates.
4 The paired, duplicate chromosomes exchange bits with one another by the process called *crossing-over*.
5 The cell divides into two daughter cells, the chromosomes separating so that each daughter cell has the same number of chromosomes as the parent cell.
6 These daughter cells divide into four granddaughter cells, each of which inherits half the number of chromosomes in the original cell.

while others get the much smaller Y chromosome – a process which is fundamental to the determination of the sex of the next generation. In man and other mammals, inheritance of two X chromosomes produces a female and inheritance of an X and a Y chromosome produces a male. In some other groups, birds for example, the opposite is the case: cock birds are XX and hen birds XY.

Meiosis is important to heredity, and so also to evolution, because it ensures that all progeny of the same parents are different. When sex cells come together in the act of fertilization, the fertilized egg will always have a new combination of chromosomes and their genes. In this way a greater variety of life is created. This variety is further enhanced during meiosis by the process of crossing over, in which the matching pairs of chromosomes exchange bits with one another before separating from one another to go individually to the sex cells.

Crossing over can be seen as a shuffling of parental genes. It helps to produce the kind of result that we all recognize when we make such observations as 'He's got his mother's eyes but his father's ears'. It also helps to explain why brothers and sisters, while usually bearing a family resemblance, are nevertheless usually recognizably different from one another. Exceptions occur, of course, when brothers or sisters are identical, as in identical twins, but these individuals have grown both from the same single fertilized egg.

ALTERNATION OF GENERATIONS
Meiosis means that some cells of an organism – the sex cells – contain half the chromosomes of others – the body cells. Normally this is not easy to see, but in some plants the two types of cell form different kinds of plant. This is called alternation of generations. For example, the cells of the fern plant, below, have the full number of chromosomes. But the fern makes its spores by meiosis, so that spore cells have half the number. A spore develops into a small plant called a prothallus, right, each cell of which also has half the number. Some of these prothallus cells develop into ova and sperms, and these come together in fertilization to create cells having the full number. From such fertilized eggs, new fern plants arise.

Finding the Genes

By the second decade of the present century, all the complicated chromosome processes had been puzzled out to give a clear picture of mitosis and meiosis. However, no one as yet had observed a gene, and the search for these elusive units of heredity went on.

To test the effects of genes, geneticists needed to make many breeding experiments, and for this purpose they required organisms that breed quickly and are not too complicated genetically so that results are more easily understood. In fact, organisms of different species vary greatly in the number of chromosomes that their cells carry. Among animals, at one end of the scale comes a roundworm parasite of horses that has only two chromosomes per body cell, while at the other end of the scale are certain butterflies with more than 400 chromosomes per body cell.

The first really successful experimental organism – other than Mendel's garden peas – was the fruit fly called *Drosophila*. This is easily bred in the laboratory, has a life cycle lasting only a few weeks, and has only eight chromosomes per body cell, or four chromosomes per sex cell. Also, it has many features of head, body and wings in which variations and abnormalities are easily recognized.

Drosophila was used by the American Thomas H. Morgan for much valuable early work in genetics. Morgan and his fellow workers studied both the visible characteristics of their fruit flies and also the features of the fruit flies' chromosomes that appeared to correspond to these characteristics. This work was continued by Hermann Muller, who used X-rays to induce in the fruit flies an increased number of the genetic changes called mutations. A catalogue of clearly recognizable mutations was thus built up, and in many cases an abnormality of the fruit flies' bodies could be correlated with a particular abnormality of a chromosome.

A further bonus to *Drosophila* work was the discovery of giant chromosomes in the fly's salivary glands. These chromosomes are so very large because they are really many identical chromosomes lined up exactly together. By staining the chromosomes suitably, the geneticists were able to see many narrow bands running across them.

These bands corresponded to very small lengths of each individual chromosome. Also, abnormalities of these bands could often be matched up precisely to abnormalities in the flies that carried the giant chromosomes. Genes had been found at last.

Below: Down's syndrome, more often called mongolism, affects about 1 in 600 children, most frequently those of older mothers. These children have an extra chromosome, No. 21 (inset).

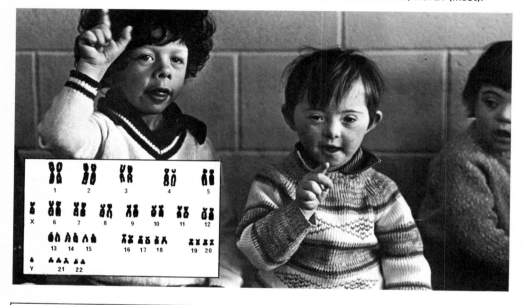

Part of a giant salivary gland chromosome

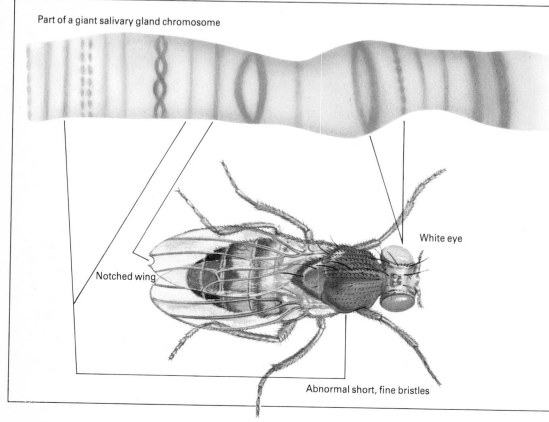

Notched wing

White eye

Abnormal short, fine bristles

Left: Various distinct bands on the giant chromosomes of the little fruit fly *Drosophila* correspond to particular hereditary abnormalities. The bands are, in fact, visible evidence of the mutated genes causing the abnormalities.

Drosophila's four pairs of chromosomes

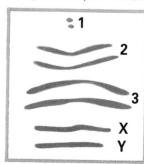

1
2
3
X
Y

Genes and DNA

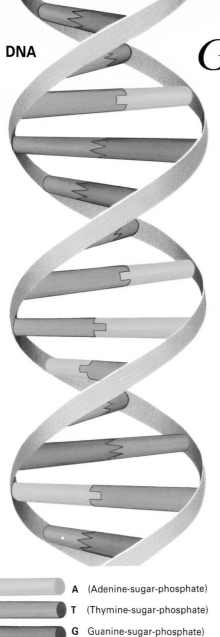

	A	(Adenine-sugar-phosphate)
	T	(Thymine-sugar-phosphate)
	G	Guanine-sugar-phosphate)
	C	(Cytosine-sugar-phosphate)

Above: The diagram shows a small part of the immensely long, complex molecule of DNA. It consists of two helical strands, wound around each other and linked together. Each strand is made up of a sequence of four chemical bases, called A, T, G and C for short. These bases are held together along the strands by chemical bonds, and further bonds between bases in opposite chains form the links that hold the chains together.

By the early 1920s, Thomas Morgan and his fellow workers had mapped large parts of the fruit fly's chromosomes to show the exact positions of many genes that caused specific effects in the fruit fly. But although many genes had been located on chromosomes, these hereditary units remained a great puzzle. No one at this time, or for 20 years afterwards, had a clear idea of what a gene actually was – of its chemical structure.

Single genes are small parts of the complete genetic material inherited by an organism. To find this genetic material itself, biochemists looked for a complex type of chemical molecule, that was made up of many simpler parts which would correspond to individual genes. Proteins, which are giant molecules made up of hundreds of smaller molecules, the amino acids, strung together, seemed good candidates. This guess, although intelligent, turned out to be wrong. In the chemistry of the living cell, the real genetic material lies behind proteins – it is the substance that prescribes how proteins are made inside living cells.

Finding the Chemical of Heredity

NUCLEIC ACID has been known for at least half a century, as a complex substance (found in the cell nucleus) which reacts as an acid and is easily made visible by staining. Chromosomes are also located in the cell nucleus, and eventually it became apparent that they were the main sites of nucleic acid. But since chromosomes also contain a good deal of protein, their nucleic acid was not at this time clearly identified as the substance of heredity.

The next major clue came in 1944, when medical bacteriologists had been working for two decades with a dangerous bacterium called *Pneumococcus*. This they grew in the laboratory on a nutrient jelly, where it formed colonies having a smooth texture. *Pneumococci* from these colonies, if inhaled, could cause a fatal pneumonia.

Pneumococcus was also known to form colonies that were much rougher in texture, the cells from which would not cause pneumonia. The genetic breakthrough came when it was discovered that the harmless, rough-colony type of *Pneumococcus* can be transformed into the dangerous, smooth-colony type by a nucleic-acid extract of the smooth-colony bacteria. This change could only be a genetic one, because it was inherited by the descendants of the transformed bacteria.

The Shape of DNA

The *Pneumococcus* nucleic-acid extract was, in fact, DNA or deoxy-ribonucleic acid. This was known to be a type of nucleic acid which is present in the nuclei and chromosomes of all living cells. DNA, then, which had been demonstrated to alter the genetic constitution of a microbe, was so far the most likely chemical of heredity. But the question remained: how could one type of chemical molecule, however complex, account for heredity in all living organisms?

The answer came in brilliant style in 1953, with the discovery of the structure of DNA by three young scientists, Francis Crick and James Watson in Cambridge and Maurice Wilkins in London. They described the enormously long DNA molecule, containing a million or more atoms, as having the shape of a double helix.

Each of the helical strands is made up of repetitions of only four different building blocks, called A, T, G and C for short. These can occur along the great length of the strands in a host of different serial arrangements. Already it is possible to see a huge number of different varieties of DNA, formed from these different arrangements.

If an organism's DNA, taken as a whole, is a specification for all of itself, then a single gene is a specification for just one bit of itself; therefore, a gene is a piece of DNA. An 'average' gene is a length of a DNA strand containing about 1000 of the chemical building blocks A, T, G and C.

Below: Experiments with *Pneumococcus*, a bacterium that causes pneumonia, first showed DNA to be connected with heredity.

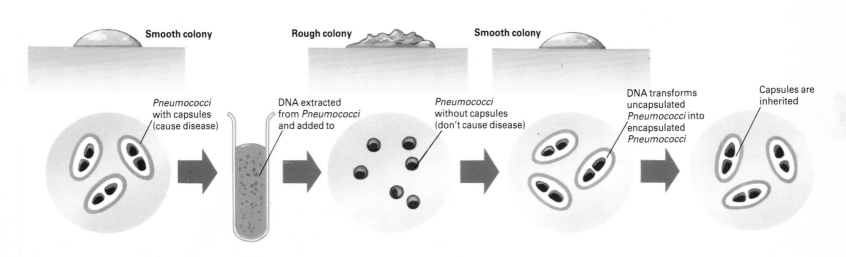

Smooth colony | Rough colony | Smooth colony

Pneumococci with capsules (cause disease)

DNA extracted from *Pneumococci* and added to

Pneumococci without capsules (don't cause disease)

DNA transforms uncapsulated *Pneumococci* into encapsulated *Pneumococci*

Capsules are inherited

Genes and Mutations

HOW DNA REPRODUCES ITSELF

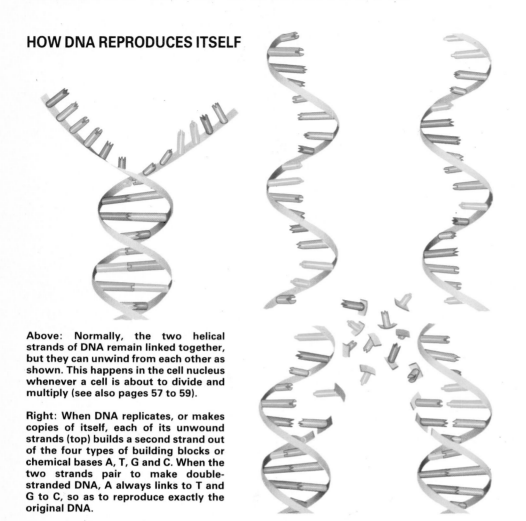

Above: Normally, the two helical strands of DNA remain linked together, but they can unwind from each other as shown. This happens in the cell nucleus whenever a cell is about to divide and multiply (see also pages 57 to 59).

Right: When DNA replicates, or makes copies of itself, each of its unwound strands (top) builds a second strand out of the four types of building blocks or chemical bases A, T, G and C. When the two strands pair to make double-stranded DNA, A always links to T and G to C, so as to reproduce exactly the original DNA.

HOW DNA MAKES A PROTEIN

m-RNA in nucleus

How proteins are made in living cells. DNA, in the nucleus, makes a molecule of m-RNA. This is an order for a particular protein, written in the language of the genetic code. The protein is built up, outside the nucleus, from amino acid sub-units. Each amino acid is supplied by a molecule of transfer-RNA (t-RNA) to which it is attached.

A genetic code word

Amino acids

t-RNA—

Start

m-RNA outside nucleus

t-RNA detaches

DNA

Amino acids link to make a protein

Stop

A gene is a length of DNA which orders the manufacture of a particular protein inside a living cell. This order or instruction is coded in the gene simply as the sequence of the four chemical building blocks, or bases, A, T, G and C, which make up the DNA molecule. More precisely, a genetic instruction is a particular sequence of genetic code words, each consisting of three chemical bases. For example, GCA and AGG are both genetic code words. There are 64 code words in all, together making up the genetic code.

The instruction for making a protein given by the gene is now copied into a message. This takes the form of another molecule of nucleic acid, called messenger-RNA, which is sent out from the nucleus to the places in the cell where proteins are made. Each code word in the messenger-RNA plays its part in the manufacture of the protein molecule, as shown in the diagram.

It can be seen that other than the code words for 'start' and 'stop', each code word of the genetic message specifies a particular amino acid, and the amino acids then get strung together to make a protein. But why is the process of protein manufacture so fundamental to life?

Versatile Proteins

The answer lies in the dual nature of proteins. One main function of proteins is body-building, although other kinds of proteins have an equally vital but entirely different function. These proteins are the body's enzymes. They are the biological CATALYSTS, which enable the tens of thousands of chemical reactions of life to take place. It is these reactions, in all their complexity, that make a host of substances inside living cells.

Mutations

An organism's genes prescribe both the development of its body and the chemical reactions by which its body works. Therefore, any 'mistake' in a gene will inevitably lead to an error in the development or functioning of the body. Such mistakes, and their consequences, are called mutations.

When a gene mutates, the mistake may be a large or a small one, but it always affects in some way the genetic code words of the gene. For example, one or more code words may be spelled wrongly, or may be missed out altogether. Mutations nearly always happen in a spontaneous manner, without any obvious cause. However, known mutagens, or causers of mutations, include radioactivity, X-rays and some chemicals.

The smallest type of mistake in a gene is the mis-spelling of a single code word. Often, this has little effect, but sometimes the changes produced can be serious, as in the hereditary defect known as sickle-cell anaemia. The mistake in question is the substitution of an A for a T, to change the single code word CTT into the incorrect CAT. CTT specifies the amino acid glutamine and CAT specifies valine. So the mutation causes the substitution of valine for the correct amino acid, glutamic acid, in the molecule of the blood protein haemoglobin.

Trivial as this mistake might seem (haemoglobin has 287 amino acids) it causes the red blood cells of an affected person to collapse into a sickle shape. The haemoglobin in these cells is also much less effective as a carrier of oxygen in the blood. Usually, any person who inherits the sickle-cell gene is at a great disadvantage and may die young. The gene would be expected to disappear from populations sooner or later, except for the rare occasion on which it would reappear because of a fresh mutation. But the sickle-cell condition also protects against the killer disease malaria, so that it has been preserved by natural selection among peoples who live in very malarial areas such as West and Central Africa.

Left: The mutation of a recessive gene for pigment formation can cause loss of pigment, or albinism. In the cat tribe, this mutation often also results in other abnormalities such as deafness and a squint. This cross-eyed tigress is a partial albino – she has reduced pigmentation and blue eyes.

INHERITANCE OF SICKLE-CELL ANAEMIA

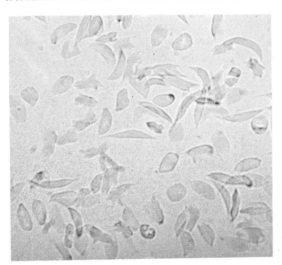

Above: In sickle-cell anaemia, the mutation of a recessive gene causes red blood cells to collapse into a sickle shape. Some normal, round red blood cells can also be seen in this photomicrograph.

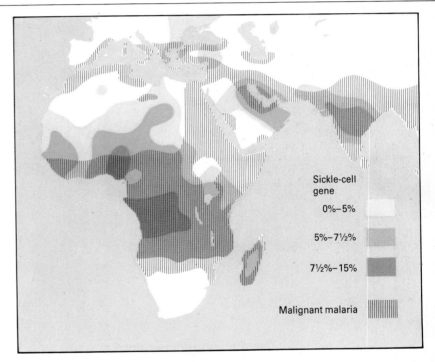

Sickle-cell gene

0%–5%

5%–7½%

7½%–15%

Malignant malaria

Above: The map shows how the malarial areas of Africa coincide with those where sickle-cell anaemia is also common.

Left: The heredity diagram shows how the sickle-cell gene is transmitted from one generation to the next. Those individuals receiving the gene from only one parent suffer no ill effects from it, and are also protected against malaria, the parasite for which lives inside red blood cells. But those individuals who get a sickle-cell gene from both parents die young from sickle-cell anaemia.

At risk — Protected

Protected — Protected

At risk — At risk

Protected

At risk — Dies young from sickle-cell anaemia

Gene for normal haemoglobin

Gene for sickle-cell haemoglobin

Chapter 5
Man versus Nature

For more than 3000 million years, life on Earth has evolved by the natural processes we have looked at briefly in this book. Throughout this vast stretch of time, the variety of life has always increased. Continually, populations of animals and plants have mingled and split apart. Time and time again, communities have invaded and conquered the territories of others, and in their turn have been conquered. Within these different populations, the hidden forces of heredity created more and more variety. The great external force of natural selection encouraged and promoted those varieties we know as evolutionary successes, and got rid of many others. The latest and biggest of evolutionary successes is man himself. But his appearance on the evolutionary scene has changed it almost out of recognition. A large part of the Earth's surface environment is now man-made. Most other living creatures must either tolerate these new conditions, or disappear – a fate already overtaking most of the larger wild animals, and many more smaller inhabitants of the disappearing rain forests. But man can also create more varieties of life, as in the new breeds of his domestic and zoo animals, and, more recently, by the scientific processes known as genetic engineering.

Among the many species domesticated by man in prehistoric times for his own use is *Allium cepa*, the onion. Modern, hybrid varieties of this plant have bulbs which are extra large and nutritious, and have no equivalent in the wild.

Man the Improver

One look at a dairy cow will show it to be a highly artificial kind of beast. In the wild, its greatly swollen udder would prove a crippling deformity. Yet in many ways the farm cow can be considered a man-made improvement over its wild ancestors.

The modern cow, like most other farm animals of today, has been produced by methods of ARTIFICIAL SELECTION or breeding. By this means domestic animals have been made to yield foods and other valuable products on a scale undreamed of by the first nomadic herders. Even the cattle of such contemporary pastoralists as the Masai, while providing tribal groups with most of their requirements, look very wasteful and unproductive beasts to local East African farmers, who have imported their own high-yielding breeding stocks from the best of Europe and India.

For similar reasons the domestic pigs of developing and developed countries are startlingly different in appearance. The Third-World village pig is a hairy, relatively lean and undersized animal, still bearing a strong resemblance to its ancestor, the forest pig or wild boar. A Western farm pig is much larger, much less hairy, and has a quite different body shape, with the weight shifted markedly towards the back — where much of the bacon comes from.

Bakewell the Breeder

Modern methods of animal breeding owe most to Robert Bakewell, an English agriculturalist of the 18th century, who improved breeds of horses and cattle, and who perfected a new and highly successful breed of sheep, the Leicestershire. Bakewell anticipated the ideas of modern genetics by establishing pure or PEDIGREE breeds, that is, animals that would breed true to type.

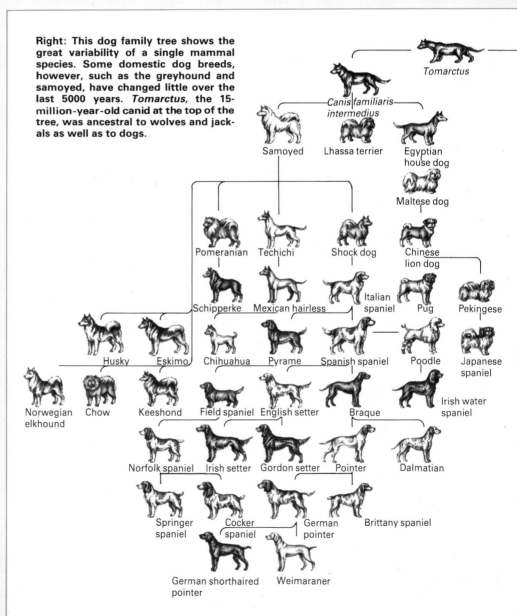

Right: This dog family tree shows the great variability of a single mammal species. Some domestic dog breeds, however, such as the greyhound and samoyed, have changed little over the last 5000 years. *Tomarctus*, the 15-million-year-old canid at the top of the tree, was ancestral to wolves and jackals as well as to dogs.

Tomarctus

Canis familiaris intermedius

Samoyed
Lhassa terrier
Egyptian house dog
Maltese dog

Pomeranian
Techichi
Shock dog
Chinese lion dog

Schipperke
Mexican hairless
Italian spaniel
Pug
Pekingese

Husky
Eskimo
Chihuahua
Pyrame
Spanish spaniel
Poodle
Japanese spaniel

Norwegian elkhound
Chow
Keeshond
Field spaniel
English setter
Braque
Irish water spaniel

Norfolk spaniel
Irish setter
Gordon setter
Pointer
Dalmatian

Springer spaniel
Cocker spaniel
German pointer
Brittany spaniel

German shorthaired pointer
Weimaraner

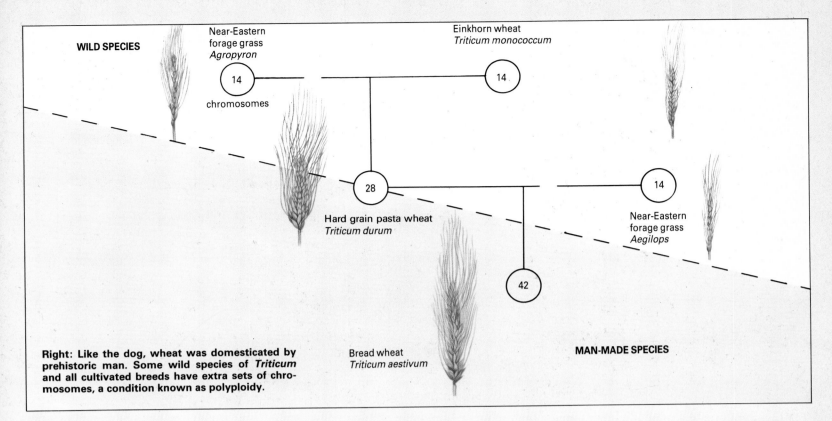

WILD SPECIES

Near-Eastern forage grass *Agropyron*

Einkhorn wheat *Triticum monococcum*

(14) chromosomes

(14)

(28)

Hard grain pasta wheat *Triticum durum*

(14)

Near-Eastern forage grass *Aegilops*

(42)

Bread wheat *Triticum aestivum*

MAN-MADE SPECIES

Right: Like the dog, wheat was domesticated by prehistoric man. Some wild species of *Triticum* and all cultivated breeds have extra sets of chromosomes, a condition known as polyploidy.

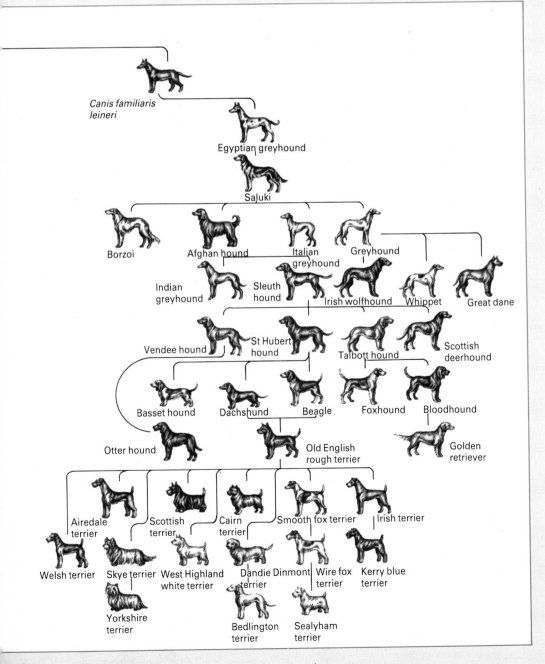

Canis familiaris leineri

Egyptian greyhound

Saluki

Borzoi — Afghan hound — Italian greyhound — Greyhound

Indian greyhound — Sleuth hound — Irish wolfhound — Whippet — Great dane

Vendee hound — St Hubert hound — Talbott hound — Scottish deerhound

Basset hound — Dachshund — Beagle — Foxhound — Bloodhound

Otter hound — Old English rough terrier — Golden retriever

Airedale terrier — Scottish terrier — Cairn terrier — Smooth fox terrier — Irish terrier

Welsh terrier — Skye terrier — West Highland white terrier — Dandie Dinmont terrier — Wire fox terrier — Kerry blue terrier

Yorkshire terrier — Bedlington terrier — Sealyham terrier

Pedigree societies, as founded by Bakewell, kept detailed records of the quality and productivity of particular animals and herds. By choosing animals of known and accredited ancestry, a breeder could then be fairly certain of good results.

Bakewell also began the system of hiring-out the services of a male stud animal for a fee. His pedigree rams then brought him not only a direct money profit, but also quickly built up sizeable herds of his sheep.

Artificial insemination is a modern extension of this idea. Semen collected from a stud animal is used to fertilize many more females than the stud male could achieve on his own, and by keeping his semen frozen alive, breeders ensure that his favourable genes can be spread long after his death.

Food Plants and Hybrids

Some of our food crops have a very long ancestry indeed. When, about 10,000 years ago, human beings first began to settle down to a life of village farming, they bred the first cereal crops, ancestors of today's wheat and barley. They selected these plants from among local wild grasses, choosing those with the largest and most nourishing seed grains. Later neolithic farmers improved these earliest cereals by cross-breeding them, sometimes with other wild grasses.

Sometimes, the progeny of such a cross would not only yield more food but would also be hardier and more disease-resistant than its parents. This type of extra hardiness is known as hybrid vigour. It results from a particular combination of favourable genes from both parents, which produce a still more favourable effect in the hybrid offspring. Hybrid vigour was the aim of many early animal- and plant-breeders, even though they had no notion of genes.

Man the Exterminator

For more than one and a half million years, since the time of his first human ancestor *Homo erectus*, man inhabited the Earth in harmony with his fellow creatures. This is not to say that he did not kill them, for from the beginning, man was a hunter. But like tribal peoples living today, prehistoric man made little impact on the total numbers of his prey species, or on most other aspects of his wider environment. Even with his extra intelligence, he remained, environmentally speaking, one animal among many others.

Things are very different today. First of all, the numbers of human beings on the Earth's surface have exploded. *Homo erectus* probably numbered at most a few millions scattered throughout the world. Even as recently as the later Middle Ages, world population numbered only a few hundred millions, whereas today it has passed the 4000 million mark and is still climbing steeply. As the most populous of the world's larger animals, man has become a threat to most of the rest.

Environmental Impact
Of course, numbers are not the whole story. Man would not be so numerous without his advanced technology, which alone can provide necessities such as food, medicines, housing and transport on the scale demanded. At an ever increasing rate, agriculture and industry are converting the natural environment into a man-made one.

For many plants and animals, urban development is not necessarily a threat. For example, in overcrowded urban England, foxes seem to be just about as common as in more rural times. Cleverly, they have chosen to become a COMMENSAL of man, feeding from the rich pickings of his dustbins. Some plants, such as the colourful rosebay willowherb, thrive on urban waste ground.

On a wider scale, however, the story is usually a much less happy one. For all the very large wild mammals, the outlook is

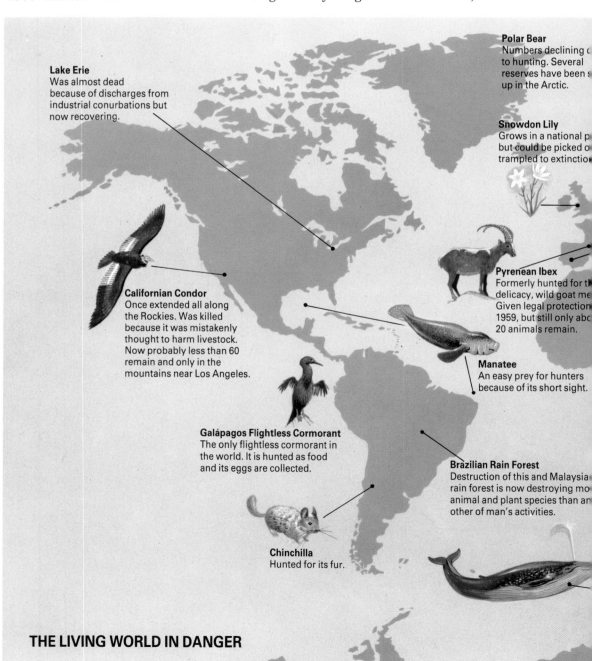

THE LIVING WORLD IN DANGER

Lake Erie
Was almost dead because of discharges from industrial conurbations but now recovering.

Californian Condor
Once extended all along the Rockies. Was killed because it was mistakenly thought to harm livestock. Now probably less than 60 remain and only in the mountains near Los Angeles.

Galápagos Flightless Cormorant
The only flightless cormorant in the world. It is hunted as food and its eggs are collected.

Chinchilla
Hunted for its fur.

Polar Bear
Numbers declining due to hunting. Several reserves have been set up in the Arctic.

Snowdon Lily
Grows in a national park but could be picked or trampled to extinction.

Pyrenean Ibex
Formerly hunted for the delicacy, wild goat meat. Given legal protection in 1959, but still only about 20 animals remain.

Manatee
An easy prey for hunters because of its short sight.

Brazilian Rain Forest
Destruction of this and Malaysian rain forest is now destroying more animal and plant species than any other of man's activities.

bleak indeed. Elephants, rhinos and hippos, because of their size and the size of their territories, have little opportunity to share in a human environment, except as zoo animals. For the great whales, which cannot be preserved even in this limited way, extinction by man may be a matter of only the next few years or decades.

Pollution Genetics

Conservation groups are rightly concerned about the threat to the quality and variety of life posed by modern technology and the pollution it causes. Although manufacturing industry is not as dirty as it once was, toxic gases and liquid effluents are still released from factories on an alarming scale, poisoning our air and water. Cars, lorries, aeroplanes and oil tankers are other major 'vehicles of pollution'. Human body wastes alone, as untreated sewage, are threatening to poison such large, confined bodies of water as the Mediterranean Sea.

To these pollutants have lately been added the RADIOACTIVE WASTES from nuclear power stations and reprocessing plants. Military technology, with its H-bomb tests, has on several occasions loaded the atmosphere with radioactivity to a dangerously high level. Not only radioactivity but many other forms of pollution can be mutagenic — causes of highly undesirable gene mutations.

Considering selfishly our own species only, it has been estimated that our chromosomes contain about 50,000 genes. If only one of these genes mutates in a body cell, the result could be cancer. If the 'hit' gene lies in our sex cells, any unfortunate consequences will be visited upon our children. The normal, average MUTATION RATE is about 1 in 50,000, so that any one of us can expect to have one mutated gene per cell. Very few mutated genes have any serious effect, but when considering any industrial or other development that could further raise the level of radioactivity or other mutagens, we should also consider the consequences of raising the mutation rate in genes from this currently low level.

Amphibians
Japanese giant salamander
Axolotl
Israel painted frog
Black toad
Seychelle Island tree frog

Birds
Galápagos penguin
Arabian ostrich
Titicaca grebe
Japanese petrel
Galápagos flightless cormorant
King shag
Short-tailed albatross
Japanese white stork
Giant ibis
Hawaiian goose or nene
Auckland Island flightless teal
Mexican duck
California condor
Galápagos hawk
Monkey-eating eagle
Spanish Imperial eagle
Everglade kite
American peregrine falcon
White-eared pheasant
Whooping crane
Siberian white crane
Auckland Island rail
Horned coot
New Zealand shore plover
Eskimo curlew
Madeira long-toed pigeon
Seychelles turtle dove
Kakapo or owl parrot
St Kilda wren
Dappled bulbul
Rufous-headed robin
Molokai thrush
Seychelles black flycatcher
Helmeted honeyeater
Crested honeycreeper
Barbados yellow warbler
Wilkin's bunting
Dusky seaside sparrow

Fish
Shortnose sturgeon
Kaluga
Mexican golden trout
Rio Grande cutthroat trout
Kern rainbow trout
Desert dace
Giant catfish
Ozark cavefish
Devils hole pupfish
Unarmoured threespine stickleback
Suwannee bass
Snail Darter

Endangered plants
More than 25,000 types of wild flowering plants are estimated to be in danger of extinction because of man's activities.

St Helena ebony
Ford's tree of Heaven
Flamboyant
Mt Athos woodruff
Jasmine-flowered heath
Mt Athos thrift
Three kings trumpet flower
Marsh rose
Blushing bride
Lady's slipper orchid
Cooktown orchid
Philippine garland-flower
Poor knights brush lily
Coco de mer
Mt Athos woad
Juno heath
Virgin everlasting

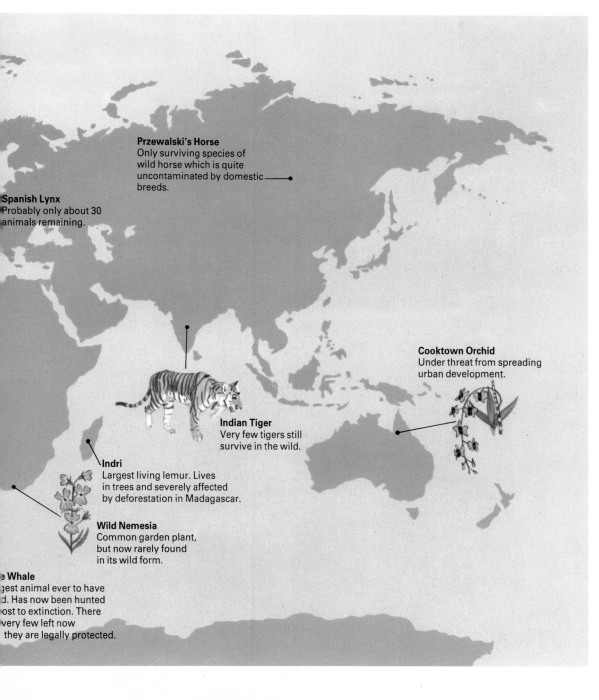

Przewalski's Horse
Only surviving species of wild horse which is quite uncontaminated by domestic breeds.

Spanish Lynx
Probably only about 30 animals remaining.

Cooktown Orchid
Under threat from spreading urban development.

Indian Tiger
Very few tigers still survive in the wild.

Indri
Largest living lemur. Lives in trees and severely affected by deforestation in Madagascar.

Wild Nemesia
Common garden plant, but now rarely found in its wild form.

Whale
gest animal ever to have d. Has now been hunted ost to extinction. There very few left now they are legally protected.

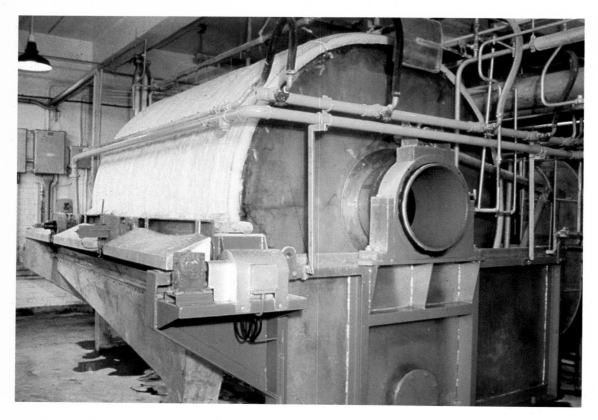

Biological Engineering

The two hundred years that ended in 1950 are famous for their great feats of engineering in such materials as iron and steel, aluminium and concrete. The two hundred years that follow this date will very likely be an age of engineering with living tissues, cells and genes. Whether we, as individuals, approve of it or not, this age of man-made evolution is already well under way. From television and radio programmes and newspaper reports it has become familiar to us in two distinct ways.

First, human beings are starting to engineer their own bodies. In transplant surgery, replacement of defective kidneys has become quite common, and routine heart and liver transplants will doubtless follow. Advances in orthopaedic surgery have led to the wholesale replacement of diseased joints. Artificial internal joints, moreover, are in some ways superior to natural ones because they cannot become arthritic or rheumatic.

The unborn human being is also beginning to be selected artificially as a 'superior product'. By amniocentesis, withdrawal of liquid surrounding the early foetus, surgeons can inspect cells and chromosomes for a number of abnormalities. Increasingly, this allows abnormal births to be prevented – always, of course, with the full agreement of the parents. By the separation of X and Y sperms, parents may soon be given the choice of a boy or girl child – although whether this would lead to evolutionary improvements is open to doubt!

In the second kind of biological engineering, scientists are manipulating the chromosomes and genes of non-human life. This, as you might suppose, can be much less controversial than human biological engineering. For example, geneticists seeking to improve the quality of cereal food plants have been able to speed up genetic experiments greatly by transplanting a cell nucleus from the ovary of one plant to that of another.

Plant geneticists are also seeking to combine the lives of cereals and other major food plants with those of the useful microbes that 'fix' nitrogen from the air. This happens naturally in such plants as beans, alfalfa and rice, but the effect of such a man-made SYMBIOSIS would be a world-wide agricultural revolution in which most food plants would make their own nitrogen fertilizers.

Tailoring the Microbe

GENETIC ENGINEERING began during World War Two with discoveries of the genetics of bacteria. A bacterium usually has only a single chromosome, which is simply a very long loop of DNA. For some bacteria, nearly all the genes on their single chromosome have now been mapped. This sort of detailed mapping allows microbial geneticists to add to, or subtract from, the genes of these microbes almost at will.

Already we employ bacteria widely as micro-machines, to carry out precise tasks in the manufacture of foodstuffs, pharmaceuticals, antibiotics, hormones and vitamins. In the near future, by building new genetic capabilities into microbes, we may also be able to use them to clean up oil spillages and other harmful wastes, and to extract underground minerals.

SELECTING MUTANT BACTERIA

A drop of culture containing a million bacteria is placed on agar, a food jelly, to which an antibiotic has been added.

In less than an hour the bacteria divide and multiply. But nearly all are killed by the antibiotic. Only one survives to grow into a single colony.

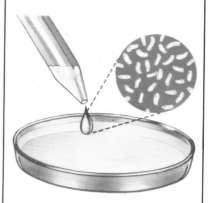

From this colony, which contains only mutant, resistant bacteria, a culture is made, and one drop is added to antibiotic agar.

This time, many colonies appear, containing billions of resistant bacteria. A new variety of organism has been bred in only a few hours.

Microbes have already been made to carry a few genes from higher organisms. In the biological industry of the future, this could mean the large-scale manufacture of human or animal metabolic products coded for by the carried genes. ANTIBODIES made in this way could be used for the creation of immunity against disease.

In a similar way, the cells of human beings and other higher organisms could be made to display many of the particular genetic talents of microbes. These might include extra capabilities for the repair of DNA-damage, or mutations. Such an advance would almost certainly mean a great breakthrough in the treatment of cancer.

Of course, man's ability to alter life – and even to create new forms of it – can also be used for evil, as in the breeding of super-virulent microbes for biological warfare, or as the accidental escape of a new, man-made virus against which there is no defence. Even when the intention is wholly good, the production of new forms or varieties of life must always be most carefully considered and controlled.

Below: Arrayed like toy models, these frogs are living multiplets produced by transplanting nuclei from the body cells of a single albino into many identical, de-nucleated egg-cells. The production of such genetically identical populations is called cloning.

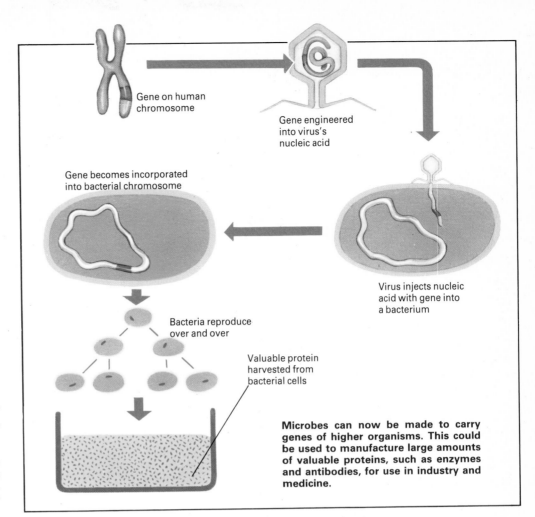

Gene on human chromosome

Gene engineered into virus's nucleic acid

Gene becomes incorporated into bacterial chromosome

Virus injects nucleic acid with gene into a bacterium

Bacteria reproduce over and over

Valuable protein harvested from bacterial cells

Microbes can now be made to carry genes of higher organisms. This could be used to manufacture large amounts of valuable proteins, such as enzymes and antibodies, for use in industry and medicine.

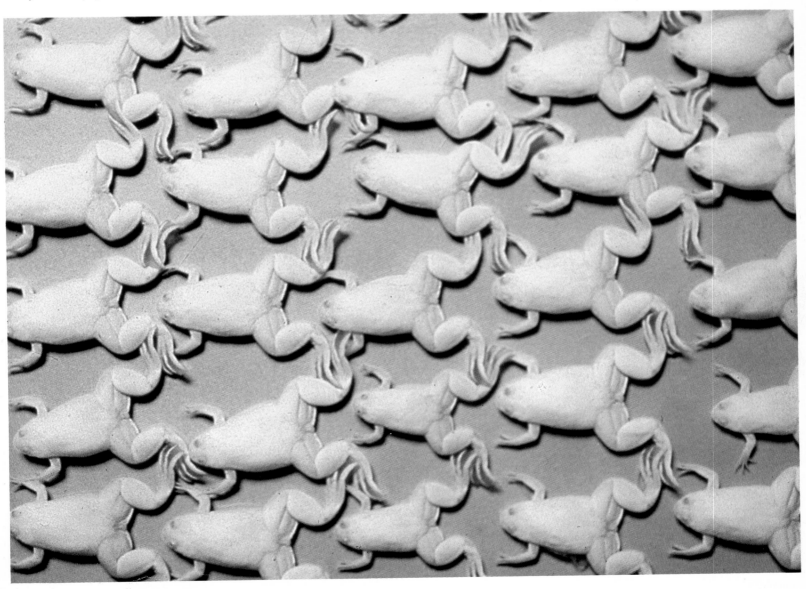

Dictionary of Evolution

A

Acquired characteristics are those obtained by a living organism during its own lifetime, not as the sole result of genetic programming but also because of interreaction with the environment. All learning, for example, is an acquired characteristic. See also LAMARCKISM.

Adaptation of a living organism is any change in its form, structure or function that makes it better suited to its environment.

Adaptive radiation is an important type of evolutionary change. It occurs when closely related species diverge into a more varied group, by progressive adaptations to different HABITATS.

Algae are extremely numerous and diverse plants, mostly living in water and ranging in size from microscopic single-cells to giant seaweeds. Even the largest algae have a relatively simple structure, lacking VASCULAR TISSUES. See also BLUE-GREEN ALGAE.

Allele is any one of the alternative forms of a particular GENE. Alleles occupy the same relative position on a CHROMOSOME and pair up during MEIOSIS. One allele can mutate into a different allele.

Alternation of generations is the appearance in succession of two genetic forms of an organism in its total life cycle. One form has DIPLOID cells, but produces HAPLOID spores. The other form, arising from the haploid spores, produces sex cells which come together in fertilization to begin the next, diploid, generation.

Altruistic behaviour is any kind of behaviour which exposes the individual animal to risk but which may protect members of the family or larger group to which the animal belongs. See also KIN SELECTION.

Amino acids are organic chemical molecules that contain both an acid and an amine (alkaline) chemical group. These two groups can react together to link one amino acid molecule with another. When many amino acid molecules are linked in this way, a protein molecule is formed. In living organisms, about 20 different amino acids occur, although chemists can make very many more kinds in the laboratory.

Ammonites are fossil molluscs, well known for their flattened, spiral-shaped shells. As living animals they flourished for about 450 million years, until the end of the Age of Reptiles 65 million years ago. Their nearest living relative, which is also a marine mollusc with a spiral shell, is the pearly nautilus.

Amphibians are an ancient group of backboned animals. Most live on land but must breed in water. Among living amphibians, frogs, toads, newts and salamanders all lay their eggs and live as tadpoles in water. A much smaller group, the caecilians, resembles earthworms and mostly burrows.

Anthropology is the scientific study of the physical, social and cultural life of man. The study of fossil man should be called palaeoanthropology.

Antibodies are very important parts of the body's natural defence system. They are produced by the body in response to infections or to the presence of other foreign substances such as vaccines and transplants. Chemically, antibodies are globular PROTEINS which circulate in the blood.

Arachnids are a class of invertebrate animals. Living members include the spiders, scorpions, mites, ticks and daddy longlegs. These are mostly small creatures, but extinct arachnids included the giant eurypterids or sea scorpions.

Arthropods form the largest phylum of invertebrate animals. They include the ARACHNIDS, INSECTS, crabs and other crustaceans, centipedes and millipedes. All have in common a hard outer body armour or exoskeleton, to which muscles and other internal parts are attached. The name arthropod refers to the many-jointed legs of these animals.

Artificial selection is the choosing and breeding by man of individual animals and plants.

Asexual reproduction is any reproductive process of a living organism which does not involve sex cells. Examples are reproduction by division of, or budding from, the parental cell or body, and reproduction from spores, which are specialized, non-sexual cells.

Atmosphere, primitive is the name given to the blanket of gases that surrounded the Earth for the first half of its life up to the present time. Most probably, the main gases present towards the end of this period were methane (CH_4), hydrogen (H_2), ammonia (NH_3), carbon dioxide (CO_2) and water vapour (H_2O). Some of these gases would have been present even before the solidification of the rocks. Others would have been added later by volcanic activity. All oxygen was locked up in the form of chemical compounds, so that the first forms of life arose independently of this gas. These primitive forms of life are today represented by anaerobic BACTERIA that live in mud, ooze and soil, for whom oxygen is a poisonous gas.

Australopithecines were man-like primates living about 5½–1½ million years ago. Many of their fossil remains have been unearthed in East Africa, notably by Dr Louis Leakey and his wife and son. These and other finds show that australopithecines existed as at least two distinct species, *Australopithecus boisei*, a robust form, and *Australopithecus africanus*, who was more slender.

Autosomes are all those CHROMOSOMES which are not sex chromosomes. Thus, a human being inherits 22 autosomes from each of his or her parents. The omission of one or more autosomes is fatal to the development of the human embryo. Extra autosomes are usually also fatal, although mongol children, born with one chromosome No. 21 too many, have a fair life expectancy.

B

Bacteria are one-celled micro-organisms which are distinguished from most other forms of single-cell life, such as microscopic ALGAE, FUNGI and PROTOZOA, by the simpler organization of their cell. For example, the NUCLEUS of a bacterium, unlike that of nearly all other types of cell, lacks an enveloping membrane. Bacteria are very diverse in their life styles. Many are PARASITES, many others are SAPROPHYTES, and yet others make their own food, either like plants with the aid of CHLOROPHYLL, or by other chemical methods.

Biochemistry is the science that deals with the many, and usually complex, chemical reactions that take place in living organisms. It can thus be regarded both as a branch of chemistry and of biology.

Biological polymers are chemical compounds which account for a large part of the structure of living matter. They are called polymers because their giant molecules are made up of many smaller molecules linked, or polymerized, together. PROTEINS are made up of many amino acid units, and polysaccharides, such as starch and CELLULOSE, are made up of many linked sugar molecules. The nucleic acids DNA and RNA are giant polymers of nitrogen bases called nucleotides. Yet other biopolymers contain various combinations of polymers, with or without fats or lipids.

Birds arose from the RULING REPTILES, and so, unlikely as it might seem, are fairly close relatives of the DINOSAURS. Modern birds, however, differ profoundly from their reptilian ancestors in their many adaptations for flight. This applies even to flightless birds such as the ostrich, which most probably have descended from flying birds, although fossil evidence for this is lacking.

Bluegreen algae are common inhabitants of soil and water. Like most other very small algae they are photosynthetic organisms containing only one, or a few, types of cell. But the structure of their cells differs profoundly from that of other algae, being generally more like that of BACTERIA. In particular, the chlorophyll pigment of a bluegreen algal cell is not packeted inside chloroplasts as in all other plants, but is distributed more widely in the cell. Ancient bluegreen algae were the organisms principally responsible for the oxygen in the Earth's atmosphere. (See also ATMOSPHERE, PRIMITIVE.)

Bony fishes include the great majority of living fishes. They are named after their bony skeleton, to distinguish them from such fishes as sharks and rays which have a skeleton of cartilage. This distinction, however, was not originally an evolutionary one, because the very first fishes, from which bony fishes and cartilaginous fishes are descended, had a bony skeleton.

Buffon, George Louis Leclerc, Comte de (1707–1788) wrote one of the first encyclopedic works on natural history, *Histoire Naturelle*. He believed in evolution and shared with his friend Lamarck the idea that ACQUIRED CHARACTERISTICS can be inherited. This idea was later elaborated by Darwin in his theory of pangenesis.

C

Cartilaginous fishes See BONY FISHES.

Catalyst is, in chemical terms, any substance that causes the speeding-up of a chemical reaction, without being changed itself in any permanent way by the reaction. Many types of catalyst, including pure metals and chemical compounds, are employed in chemical manufacture. For biological catalysts, see ENZYMES.

Cellulose is a natural polymer, a giant molecule which is made up of thousands of linked molecules of the sugar glucose. The stiff outer walls of plant cells, which most clearly distinguish these from animal cells, are made from cellulose. Cotton fibres are nearly pure cellulose.

Chlorophyll is the green pigment of plants, by which they are enabled to make their own food by PHOTOSYNTHESIS. In the cells of green leaves and stems of plants, chlorophyll is contained within small packets called chloroplasts. In the cells of BLUEGREEN ALGAE and photosynthetic BACTERIA, chlorophyll is more widely distributed.

Chordates are animals that belong to the great group or phylum Chordata, which includes the VERTEBRATES. All chordates, at one time or another in their lives, possess a notochord, a rigid cellular rod, situated dorsally, which is the main internal support of the body. In vertebrates the notochord is present only in embryonic life, its function later being taken over by the backbone. Besides vertebrates, chordates include *Amphioxus*, the lancelet.

Chromosomes are microscopic, elongated bodies, present in the cell NUCLEUS, that carry the genes, or units of heredity. The chromosomes of bacteria, normally only one to each cell, are long loops of DNA. The chromosomes of all higher forms of cell, usually several or many to each cell, are more complex, containing PROTEINS as well as DNA.

Classification divides organisms into groups, usually by their structure. What we recognize as a sort of animal or plant is generally a particular SPECIES. A species has two Latin names; the first is the GENUS, which may be shared by several or many species, and the second is the name for the particular species. Just as species are grouped in genera, so genera are grouped into a family and families into an order. Orders in turn are grouped in a class, classes in a phylum, and phyla in a kingdom. So the domestic cat, *Felis catus*, is a member of the cat family (Felidae), in the order Carnivora, or meat-eaters. Carnivores are one of the orders in the class Mammalia, and mammals are a class in the phylum of chordates, part of the animal kingdom.

Codon is the technical name for a genetic code word. It comprises a sequence of three nucleotide bases in a molecule of DNA or RNA. A codon generally is an 'order' for a particular AMINO ACID to be incorporated into a PROTEIN molecule. An *anticodon* is a sequence of three nucleotide bases that links up specifically with a codon. Each molecule of RNA (t-RNA) that carries an amino acid for protein synthesis, contains a particular anticodon.

Coelacanths are LOBEFINNED FISHES, all of which were supposed to be long extinct until, in 1938, the first living coelacanth was caught in deep waters off the South African coast. Coelacanths are of great evolutionary interest because they are very close relatives of the first land VERTEBRATES. This is shown, for example, by the arrangement of bones inside their lobed fins, which clearly resembles that of the five-digit hand and foot.

Colony has a number of distinct meanings in biology. A bacterial colony is a visible aggregation containing thousands, or even millions, of invisibly small BACTERIA. A coral reef contains many colonies of small coral animals, all physically linked together in their colonies as group organisms. Colonial insects such as bees, wasps, ants and termites construct a nest or colony in which they live a complex social life together.

Commensalism means, roughly, eating at the same table. It describes an association between two or more different organisms whereby they share food and a general environment without the vital need to do so. Man and mouse, and hermit crab and sea anemone, are two examples of commensal partnership.

Convergent evolution refers either to a close resemblance between species that are not closely related (for example, mole and marsupial mole), or to the resemblance of individual features or organs of unrelated species (for example, the eye of vertebrates and the eye of cephalopods such as squids and octopuses).

Creodonts were primitive carnivorous land mammals that lived about 65–25 million years ago. They gave rise to such modern carnivores as cats, dogs, bears, racoons, civets, hyenas and weasels and their allies, as well as to seals, sealions, walruses and possibly whales.

Cryptic coloration is one kind of camouflage, a coloration which makes an animal inconspicuous to its predators or prey. The stripes of the tiger are a well-known example.

Cuvier, Georges Leopold, Baron (1769–1832) was the most eminent of French naturalists in the early 19th century. He was anti-evolutionist, believing that species periodically become extinct because of catastrophes, whereupon more species are created anew. He also believed that each animal organ is untransmutable, having been created for a particular function and no other. He was scathing about Lamarck's notion of evolutionary change proceeding by the inheritance of ACQUIRED CHARACTERISTICS, regarding this idea (with some reason) as based on too little evidence.

D

Darwin, Charles Robert (1809–1882) published *On the Origin of Species by Means of Natural Selection* in 1859. His other important works include *The Variation of Animals and Plants under Domestication* (1868), in which he attempted to account for heredity by his theory of pangenesis; *The Descent of Man, and Selection in Relation to Sex* (1871); *The Expression of the Emotions in Man and Animals* (1872); and a number of later works on plant breeding and soil fertility which were the results of his painstaking work in the greenhouses and garden of Down House, his home in Kent.

Devonian Period is named after the Old Red Sandstone of Devon, which dates from this geological period. It is also often called the Age of Fishes because during its 50 million years, starting some 395 million years ago, first flourished most of the groups of fishes we know today, together with other groups that have since become extinct. Before the end of the Devonian, the first seed plants had evolved on land and amphibians and land invertebrates were widespread.

Dinosaurs are the most famous of the archosaurs or RULING REPTILES, which for well over 100 million years were the dominant land animals. The rep-

tile ancestors of dinosaurs, and also of their near relatives the crocodiles and the birds, were small running reptiles called thecodonts. Actually, dinosaurs were not one but two groups of reptiles, distinguished by the different shapes of their hip bone. 'Bird-hipped' dinosaurs (not the ancestors of birds) included the huge *Stegosaurus* and the duck-billed, horned and other armoured dinosaurs. 'Reptile-hipped' dinosaurs included the vast early plant-eaters and the ostrich-like and great flesh-eating dinosaurs.

Diploid cells are those having a double set of CHROMOSOMES, as, for example, all the cells of our bodies except our sex cells. Diploid cells give rise to HAPLOID cells by the process called MEIOSIS.

DNA (deoxyribonucleic acid) is a NUCLEIC ACID which contains the sugar deoxyribose. In living cells it is found mainly in the CHROMOSOMES, where it specifies genetic information for the transmission and development of all hereditary characteristics. See also RNA.

DNA repair is the name given to ENZYME processes by which certain mutations in chromosomal DNA can be reversed. For example, by a common type of mutation, thymine (T) bases situated in opposite strands of a DNA molecule become linked together to form 'thymine dimers'. This defect is repaired by an enzyme which breaks the chemical linkages, so correcting errors in the genetic code on the DNA.

Dominance has two quite distinct meanings in biology. In genetics, a dominant gene is one that will be expressed even if it is inherited from one parent only. Thus, a child that inherits a dominant gene for brown eyes from one parent and a RECESSIVE gene for blue eyes from the other parent, will be brown-eyed. In the science of animal behaviour (ethology) dominance refers to the rank of an animal within its herd or other group. Some animals are dominant over others, which are said to be subordinate or of lower rank.

E

East African anthropology has been the source of most of our present knowledge of man's immediate ancestors. The first australopithecine FOSSIL, the Taung skull, was, however, found in South Africa in 1924. In the decades following World War Two, many more comparable HOMINID fossils have been discovered in Tanzania, Kenya and Ethiopia. Most of these finds have been australopithecines, prehuman hominids dating between 5½–1½ million years ago. At the end of this period, truly human fossils and artefacts begin to appear, although a few much more problematic *Homo* fossils seem to be 3 million or more years old.

Echinoderms are the starfishes, serpent stars, sea urchins, sea lilies and sea cucumbers. The bodies of all these marine INVERTEBRATES are built on a radial plan. Other peculiar features include a system of pressurized water tubes which aid in movement. These and other features show that the history of echinoderms goes back very early in the evolution of invertebrate animals.

Environment refers to all the conditions and influences that can affect the life of an organism. Thus, an organism has an external environment – its total surroundings, including any other organisms – and an internal environment – the physical and chemical working of its body.

Environmental niche is the place in nature occupied by a species. It includes the organism's habitat and the special way the organism uses it. Two species cannot share an identical niche.

Enzymes are proteins that act inside living cells as vital organic CATALYSTS. Most enzymes catalyze only a particular chemical reaction, so that many different enzymes are needed for all an organism's chemical reactions. Enzymes do their work only within the narrow range of temperature, salt concentration, and so on, that is characteristic of living processes, and they are quickly inactivated by excessive heat and cold and by many poisons.

Eocene epoch dated between 54 and 36 million years ago. Most modern forms of life, including many groups of flowering plants and PLACENTAL

MAMMALS, were well established by this time.

F

Fitness in evolutionary terms is the biological success of an organism. This can be measured as reproductive success, that is, the number of progeny over many generations. In the individual organism, however, fitness is measured as the frequency with which particular genes are passed on to the next generation. See also GENOTYPE and PHENOTYPE.

Fossils are best known as the petrified, or stony, remains of ancient forms of life. These were formed in the rocks by processes of sedimentation which slowly replaced hard parts such as the animal skeleton and shell with mineral substances. Other stony fossils are hollow casts or impressions, which include fossil tracks and footprints. Unpetrified fossils include streaks and films of carbon; whole insects preserved in amber; and the bodies of large, extinct animals such as mammoths, preserved intact in the permanently frozen soil of Alaska and Siberia.

Fungi are familiar to most people as mushrooms, toadstools, yeasts and moulds. In fact, they are a tremendously diverse group of organisms, numbering about 50,000 species. In some ways fungi resemble simple plants, but all fungi lack the green plant pigment CHLOROPHYLL. Many fungi are PARASITES, particularly of plants. Many others are SAPROPHYTES feeding on non-living organic matter. In lichens, fungi live as symbiotic partners with single-cell algae.

G

Genes are the units by which hereditary characteristics are transmitted and determined. In general, a gene can be defined as a portion of a molecule of DNA in a CHROMOSOME inside the NUCLEUS of a living cell. In a virus, however, a gene may be either DNA or RNA.

Gene pool is the totality of genes possessed by a SPECIES. All combinations of these genes are theoretically possible through matings between different individuals of the species.

Genetics is the scientific study of heredity.

Genetic engineering is the manipulation of CHROMOSOMES and their genes to produce living organisms having novel, and possibly useful, hereditary characteristics.

Genotype is an organism described in terms of its particular set of genes. In all questions of an organism's heredity it is its genotype that is considered. See also PHENOTYPE.

Genus is a biological category containing one or more SPECIES. Examples are *Felis*, *Rosa* and *Bacillus*.

Geological evolution refers to all the changes that have taken place in the rocks of the Earth's crust since the time of their first cooling, 4000 million years ago.

H

Habitat of an organism is the particular part of the environment that it occupies, for example, sea floor, acid bog or treetop.

Haemoglobin is the red pigment of blood, carried by red blood cells. It is a protein containing an iron group (haem) that binds to oxygen, which it carries to all living cells of the body. Haemoglobin also transports some waste carbon dioxide from tissues to lungs.

Haploid cells are those having a single set of CHROMOSOMES. Examples are sex cells such as sperms and ova, which come together during fertilization to create a DIPLOID cell called the fertilized egg or zygote. See also ALTERNATION OF GENERATIONS.

Heterozygote is the technical term for an organism that has inherited different forms, or ALLELES, of a GENE from its parents – for example, a dominant and a recessive allele. Such organisms will not breed true for the hereditary character in question.

Hominids are members of man's own family. They include, besides *Homo sapiens* or modern man, extinct species of the genera *Homo, Australopithecus* and *RAMAPITHECUS*.

Homozygote is the technical term for an organism that has inherited similar forms, or ALLELES, of a GENE from its parents – for example, two dominant or two recessive alleles. Such organisms breed true for the hereditary character in question. Domestic animals and plants of this kind are called pure-breds.

I

Insects are the most numerous and successful of all INVERTEBRATES, with more than 750,000 species living in all parts of the world. They include the only invertebrate animals with wings. They can be distinguished from their fellow ARTHROPODS by such characters as the three pairs of legs, one pair of antennae, and the division of the body into three parts: head, thorax and abdomen.

Invertebrates are animals which do not have a backbone. They comprise the vast majority of animal species, and range in complexity from simple, wormlike creatures having only a few cells, to such advanced forms of life as insects and octopuses.

K, L

Kin selection is a form of NATURAL SELECTION that favours the family rather than the individual. It includes the selection of ALTRUISTIC BEHAVIOUR patterns, and also the selection which has produced, among social insects such as bees, sterile female workers who have 'given up' the opportunity of passing on their own genes, for the benefit of their sisters.

Lamarckism is the name given to the evolutionary ideas of the French naturalist Jean Baptiste de Lamarck (1744–1829). Lamarck saw that a study of fossils can reveal ways in which animals have undergone evolutionary change over many generations. This belief contradicted the creationism of such eminent contemporaries as CUVIER. But Lamarck also believed that evolution proceeds by the inheritance of characteristics acquired by individual animals during their own lifetimes. Modern genetics effectively contradicts this idea, so that Lamarckism is no longer seriously considered as a theory of evolution.

Larvae are juveniles of animal species which differ greatly in appearance from their adults, for example, insect grubs and caterpillars. Immature insects which look more like their adults are often called nymphs, as in dragonflies and mayflies.

Living fossil refers in general to an animal or plant species that in the course of evolution has long outlasted the rest of its group into the present time.

Lobefinned fishes are a largely extinct group of bony fishes. They are represented today only by three genera of lungfishes, and by the single known living species of coelacanth. Very closely related to the coelacanths were a third branch of lobefins, the rhipidistians, which gave rise to the first land vertebrates, the amphibians.

M

Malthus, Thomas Robert (1766–1834) was the British economist whose influential *Essay on Population* helped lead Charles Darwin to the idea of NATURAL SELECTION.

Mammals are now known to have evolved from REPTILES as long ago as 200 million years, at the time of the first DINOSAURS. They became the dominant land animals only 140 million years later, after the extinction of the great reptiles. The earliest mammals are known mostly from their teeth, which are much more varied than those of reptiles. Mammal contemporaries of the dinosaurs were mainly small, shrew-like creatures.

Mammal-like reptiles lived about 280–200 million years ago. They were distinguished from other reptiles of their time by their less sprawling gait. Later forms called therapsids actually gave rise to the mammals, and possibly had such mammalian features as body hair.

Marsupials are the pouched mammals. Like the first PLACENTAL MAMMALS, they probably descended from the pantotheres, a mammal group that became extinct about 135 million years ago.

Meiosis is the process in which, by two successive divisions of a cell NUCLEUS, the number of CHROMOSOMES in the nuclei of daughter cells is halved. It is the process by which sex cells, or gametes, are formed.

Mendel, Gregor Johann (1812–1884) was the discoverer of the laws of heredity. His revolutionary work on the genetics of peas, published in 1865, went almost unnoticed, but was rediscovered in 1900 by three botanists, H. de Vries, K. E. Correns and E. T. von Seysenegg, who were searching the literature for confirmation of their own genetic experiments.

Microfossils are the geological remains of microscopic organisms. They include fossils of the most ancient of all known living organisms, BACTERIA and BLUEGREEN ALGAE of the Fig Tree Cherts, which are about 3100 million years old.

Miller, Dr Stanley L. (1930–   ) is an American chemist who made experiments in 1953 to test the PRIMEVAL SOUP hypothesis of the origin of life. See also OPARIN and UREY.

Mimicry is a similarity in appearance between different species, which is advantageous to one or more of the species. It takes several distinct forms. An edible insect may gain protection by mimicking the bright WARNING COLORATION of a distasteful one (Batesian mimicry). Or, various distasteful insects may share a type of warning coloration that protects them equally against birds, who soon learn to avoid all such insects (Müllerian mimicry). Among plants, notable examples of mimicry are those of the bee and fly orchids, which resemble the females of those insects, and are pollinated by male insects seeking to copulate with them.

Missing link originally meant an animal that is intermediate in development between man and the great apes. No such creature has ever been discovered, but missing links have turned up to bridge the gap between other living groups. Perhaps the best example is *Peripatus*, which is intermediate between annelid worms and arthropods.

Mitochondria are minute bodies within living cells. Oxygen is metabolized inside them with the release of chemical energy. These 'powerhouses' of the cell are thought to have arisen as internal symbionts, which evolved to their present form by a process of simplification.

Mitosis is the process by which animal and plant cells divide and multiply. CHROMOSOMES in the cell NUCLEUS duplicate, after which the two diploid sets of chromosomes move apart and each becomes incorporated in the nucleus of one of the two daughter cells.

Molecular biology is the study of the structure and properties of the chemical molecules which make up living matter. As a young branch of biological science, it took a great leap forward in 1953, with the discovery of the double-helix structure of DNA.

Monotremes are the egg-laying mammals, represented today only by the platypus and *Echidna* of Australasia. Monotremes probably descended from the docodonts, a mammal group that became extinct about 140 million years ago without, apparently, giving rise to any other types of mammal.

Mutation is a sudden change in the hereditary material of an organism. If the mutation occurs within a GENE it is called a point mutation. If it involves the loss, reversal, exchange or duplication of a larger part of a CHROMOSOME, it is called a chromosome mutation. Mutations are the ultimate cause of all variety in living organisms.

Mutation rate is the average frequency of occurrence of a mutation in a population. This varies for different types of mutation, but a gene rarely mutates at a rate greater than 1 to 50,000 unless exposed to abnormally high levels of radiation or other mutagens.

N

Natural selection is the process first described by DARWIN and WALLACE to explain evolutionary change. In a population of living organisms, those individuals having characteristics which make them most suited to their environment, will leave more progeny than those less well suited. The progeny, inheriting their parents' characteristics, will similarly be subjected to natural selection, so that over many generations the individuals within a population, by becoming better and better adapted to their environment, can differ more and more from members of the original population.

Neoteny occurs when juvenile characteristics of an animal are retained into its adult life. Examples are the ostrich's fluffy chick feathers and the human being's large head (corresponding to a baby ape's). See also PAEDOGENESIS.

Nitrogen fixation is any chemical process which incorporates nitrogen from the atmosphere into chemical compounds. In nature only certain organisms have the ability to fix this very unreactive gas, so that it becomes available as a plant food. These organisms include a number of bluegreen algae and bacteria, some of which live free in soil and water, while others live as symbionts, for example the bacteria found in root nodules of members of the pea family.

Nucleic acids are complex organic chemical compounds having long, helical molecules, found in living cells and in viruses. Each strand of a nucleic acid molecule consists of a chain of linked subunits called nucleotides. Each nucleotide contains a nitrogen base, a sugar and a phosphate group. In double-stranded nucleic acids links also exist between nitrogen bases lying opposite one another on the two strands. See also DNA and RNA.

Nucleus is the headquarters or control centre of the living cell. It contains the cell's genetic material, in the form of CHROMOSOMES and their GENES. The nucleus of an animal or plant cell appears under the microscope as a rounded body, situated centrally or to one side of the cell. The nucleus of a bacterial cell appears as a diffuse patch.

O

Oparin, A. I. (1894–   ) is a Russian scientist who, in 1924, first put forward the idea that life on Earth arose from non-living matter, which itself was formed by chemical reactions between dissolved gases from the Earth's primitive atmosphere. Oparin also speculated that the first organisms could have taken the form of carbon compounds in colloid form (coacervates). These could, for example, have arisen as films coated on wet clay.

Ozone is a form of oxygen having the molecular formula O_3. It is a pale blue, unstable gas which is made from atmospheric oxygen (O_2) by hard ULTRAVIOLET RADIATION from the Sun and by electrical discharges during storms.

P

Paedogenesis is the reproduction of an animal while it is still a larva or other juvenile form. The best-known examples are certain amphibian and midge larvae, from which further larvae develop directly. In the remote past, paedogenesis could have given rise to the backboned animals, by the reproduction of some CHORDATE larva resembling the tadpole-like larva of the sea squirt.

Parasites are organisms that live and feed in or on the living bodies of other organisms, so causing their hosts harm. Parasitism is a major mode of life and examples of parasites occur throughout the animal, plant and microbial kingdoms.

Pedigree is a record of hereditary descent, for example that of a PURE-BRED animal. The term is also used to describe such animals, as in pedigree dog and pedigree herd.

Phenotype is an organism described in terms of its appearance and other generally observable characteristics. That is, it is what we usually recognize as a particular organism. Natural selection acts on phenotypes, but heredity is determined by GENOTYPES.

Photosynthesis is the process by which organisms that have the green pigment CHLOROPHYLL make their own food from carbon dioxide and water, using the energy of sunlight. The first chemical products of photosynthesis are sugars, which in green plants are further built up into starch and CELLULOSE. Photosynthetic organisms also include the Green bacteria and the Purple bacteria, today's representatives of some of the earliest of living cells.

Pineal body is a small organ situated on the roof of the vertebrate brain. In some cold-blooded animals, for example the tuatara and the lamprey, it functions as a third eye.

Placental mammals are those in which the unborn young are nourished by substances passed from the mothers' blood through an organ called the placenta. They include the vast majority of mammals outside Australasia.

Polygenes are many GENES acting together to produce their effects. All characteristics which show a continuous range of variation between extremes, such as the height and weight of human beings, are controlled by polygenes. However, no real distinction exists between a polygene and other genes, because one and the same gene can play its part in continuous variation and also produce a single, major effect.

Polymorphism refers to a number of different forms or patterns of individuals within a single species. Examples include the social insects, such as bees and termites, which have several castes with bodies of different shapes and sizes. The wings of a species of butterfly or moth may show a range of different patterns (see VARIETIES). In sexual dimorphism, male and female animals of a species differ markedly from one another.

Polyploid organisms have three or more sets of chromosomes in the nucleus of each of their body cells. Polyploidy is rare in animals but widespread among plants. Roses, for example, commonly have four, six or eight sets of chromosomes per cell.

Primates are mammals of man's own Order. They include – besides man – apes, monkeys, tarsiers, lemurs and tree shrews.

Primeval soup is the name coined for a hypothetical first form of life on Earth. This was a concentration of giant polymer molecules in water. These reproduced themselves with the aid of other chemical compounds present (their food) rather in the way that the giant polymer DNA replicates itself in living cells.

Proteins are organic chemical compounds having giant molecules made up of many AMINO ACID sub-units strung together. They perform many functions in living cells and tissues, both structurally as in muscle and connective tissue, and also in the forms of ENZYMES, ANTIBODIES and some hormones.

Protoplasm is the material of living cells. It comprises the NUCLEUS or nuclei of a cell and the surrounding, more liquid, cytoplasm.

Protozoa are single-cell organisms, mostly of microscopic size although a few have shells visible to the naked eye. They are distinguished from BACTERIA by the greater complexity of their cell. Protozoa are very varied in appearance and habit, many being free-living inhabitants of seas and inland waters, while many others live as parasites in other organisms.

Pure-breds are animals and plants whose characteristics have been maintained so that these are passed on reliably to later generations. See also HOMOZYGOTE.

R

Radioactive wastes are substances left over from nuclear explosions and nuclear industry. All radioactive substances slowly give off radiant energy which is dangerous, because it interferes with CHROMOSOMES to cause MUTATIONS. There is no way to speed up this loss of energy. The wastes must be safely stored where they cannot threaten

life, but they will be dangerous for many thousands of years.

Ramapithecus is thought to be the oldest primate that resembles man more than man's nearest relatives, the great apes. It lived about 14 million years ago. See also HOMINIDS.

Recessive gene is a gene that will only show its effects when it is inherited from both parents, or when it is carried on the X chromosome and is not paired with a corresponding gene on the Y chromosome. See also DOMINANCE and SEX-LINKED INHERITANCE.

Reptiles arose from the AMPHIBIANS about 340 million years ago. They were the first true land animals, laying thick-shelled eggs which made them independent of water for their reproductive stages. For more than 200 million years, until the fall of the DINOSAURS 70 million years ago, they were the dominant large land animals.

Rhizoids are rootlike organs that serve to hold many simpler kinds of plants to the surfaces from which they grow. But rhizoids lack the complex structure of roots associated with the taking-in and conduction of mineral nutrients.

RNA (ribonucleic acid) is a form of NUCLEIC ACID which contains the sugar ribose. Living cells contain three types, all of which are vital to the synthesis of proteins in the cell. Messenger (m–) RNA carries genetic information from the cell's DNA to sites in the cell where ribosomal (r–) RNA also assists in the building of proteins. These are built with amino acid molecules, which are brought in individually by molecules of transfer (t–) RNA. Some viruses possess RNA as their sole genetic material.

Ruling reptiles were a large and diverse group that sprang from small running reptiles called thecodonts and, during a period of 100 million years, radiated to produce the dinosaurs, the pterosaurs or flying reptiles, the crocodiles and the early birds.

S

Salamanders and newts are tailed AMPHIBIANS. Salamanders have rounded tails and as adults spend most of their time on land. Newts have flattened tails and are generally found in water.

Saprophytes are organisms that feed on non-living organic matter. They are widespread and of great importance in nature, including the bacteria and fungi that bring about decay and so recycle nutrients to the soil.

Sex-linked inheritance is the inheritance of a RECESSIVE GENE carried on the X CHROMOSOME. In male mammals the X chromosome is paired with the much smaller Y chromosome, which contains few genes, so that the recessive gene can show its effects even though it is inherited from one parent only. Since it is the mother that provides the X chromosome to her sons, sex-linked characteristics are passed on through the female line. These characteristics include such defects as red-green colour blindness and haemophilia. Because a woman inherits an X chromosome from both parents, she can only suffer from such defects if both of her parents possess the recessive gene. In birds, the whole situation is reversed because females are XY and males XX.

Sexual reproduction is reproduction of living organisms by means of gametes, or sex cells. Gametes from both parents come together to produce fertilized eggs, or zygotes, which then develop into individuals of the next generation. See also ASEXUAL REPRODUCTION.

Species is a group of freely interbreeding organisms. Among familiar animals a species is what we recognize as a particular kind of animal, for example the domestic cat, *FELIS CATUS*. Here, *CATUS* is the species name which tells us that it is a domestic cat and no other. See also CLASSIFICATION.

Survival of the fittest and struggle for existence are phrases coined in the 19th century to express DARWIN'S and WALLACE'S theory of NATURAL SELECTION in terms that were generally understandable.

Symbiosis is an association between two organisms of different species, from which both partners benefit. Examples are widespread in nature. Sometimes the two organisms are clearly distin-

guishable from one another, as in the case of the tick bird and the rhino. In other cases they are very intimately associated, as in the fungus and alga which together make a lichen.

T

Territory of an animal is the place it occupies, together with its family, within its general HABITAT. Other individuals of the same species which trespass in an animal's territory are usually attacked. This kind of territorial behaviour is common among all groups of vertebrate animals.

Trilobites were marine ARTHROPODS that left a long and varied fossil record. They lived about 570–270 million years ago and numbered at least 1000 different genera, which geologists find very useful in dating Cambrian rocks.

U

Ultraviolet radiation has wavelengths and a penetrating ability intermediate between those of visible light and those of X-rays. Longer-waved, or soft, ultraviolet rays reach us from the Sun – for example, they are the rays in sunlight which tan our bodies. Shorter-waved, or hard, ultraviolet rays are harmful to us but are trapped in the upper atmosphere.

Urey, Harold Clayton (1893–   ) is an American chemist who in 1952 theoretically confirmed the ideas of A. I. OPARIN on the nature of the Earth's ancient atmosphere. See ATMOSPHERE, PRIMITIVE.

V

Variations in biological terms are differences between individual organisms. They can be the result of environmental conditions acting on an inherited disposition, for example the different colours of a stoat's fur in summer and winter. Or, the differences can be inherited entirely, as are our own facial features, by which others recognize us individually. New variations appear in nature as the result of the NATURAL SELECTION of favourable MUTATIONS.

Varieties in biological classification are groups within a single species that have distinct features, for example particular patterns, colours or body shapes.

Vascular tissues in plants are those which conduct liquid food substances through the plant. Phloem consists of living cells which conduct solutions of various organic substances and mineral salts. Xylem consists of non-living, woody, tubes that conduct water and salts.

Vertebrates are animals with backbones. They comprise fishes, amphibians, reptiles, birds and mammals. See also CHORDATES, INVERTEBRATES.

Viruses are non-cellular micro-organisms, mostly very much smaller than bacteria. They reproduce, or replicate, only within living cells, sometimes, but not always, causing disease in their hosts, which can be any other form of life on Earth. (Viruses themselves can be considered as living or non-living.) The smallest and simplest viruses consist only of a protein capsule which encloses a NUCLEIC ACID, which may be DNA or RNA. Larger viruses have a more complex constitution but no virus is as complex as a living cell. The evolution of viruses is a puzzle – it is unlikely that they are ancestral to cells. In some ways they resemble escaped genes.

W

Wallace, Alfred Russell (1823–1913) was co-discoverer, with Charles Darwin, of NATURAL SELECTION.

Warning coloration refers to the bright colours, such as black-and-yellow, or black-and-orange, shown by many animals, particularly insects and amphibians. These colours serve to warn birds and other predators that the animal in question is distasteful or poisonous. See also MIMICRY.

Index

ACKNOWLEDGEMENTS
Picture Research: Elizabeth Rudoff

Photographs: 6 E.S Bargdoarn/Harvard University left, Brian Hawkes right; 7 ZEFA/E. Hummel top left, Heather Angel bottom left, N.H.P.A./Douglas Dickens top right, ZEFA/B. Fleumer bottom right; 8–9 Ardea Photographics/Adrian Warren; 10 Royal College of Surgeons; 11 Seaphot/Rod Salm; 12 Stirling Photographic top, Heather Angel bottom; 13 South African Tourist Agency; 14–15 ZEFA/E. Hummel; 15 G. R. Roberts left, Heather Angel right; 16–17 Heather Angel; 18 E. S. Bargdoarn/Harvard University; 19 Oxford Scientific Films top, N.H.P.A./M. Walker bottom; 21 Seaphot/Christian Petron top, Heather Angel centre left, right; 24 Heather Angel; 25 Ardea Photographics; 27 N.H.P.A./I. Polunin; 31 Brian Hawkes; 32 Imitor; 32/33 N.H.P.A./Philip Wayne; 33 G. R. Roberts; 34 Zoological Society of London; 36–37 N.H.P.A.; 38, 39 Heather Angel top centre, bottom right, Marion Morrison top right, P. Morris, bottom centre; 40, 41 Heather Angel top right, Natural Science Photos/C. A. Walker centre right, P. Morris bottom; 42 A. Bannister top left, centre, Zoological Society of London bottom left, ZEFA/Ziesmann bottom right; 44 Seaphot/Adrian Stevens; 44–45 ZEFA/Leidmann; 46 N.H.P.A./M. Morcombe top, Bruce Coleman bottom; 47 Reinhard-Tierfoto; 49 Zoological Society of London top, N.H.P.A./Douglas Dickens centre; 50 N.H.P.A./M. W. F. Tweedie top, Heather Angel centre, bottom; 51 Heather Angel top, P. Morris centre, N.H.P.A./Walker bottom; 52–53 Harry Smith; 54–55 N.H.P.A./E. A. James; 56 Alan Hutchison top, Syndication International Ltd bottom; 57 Gene Cox top right, South African Tourist Agency bottom left, ZEFA bottom right; 58 Institute of Ophthalmology/G. M. Villermet; 59 Heather Angel; 60 National Society for Mentally Handicapped Children; 63 National Zoological Park, Washington, D.C. top, University College Hospital centre; 64–65 ZEFA/B. Fleumer; 66 N.H.P.A./E. Hanumantha; 66–67 Bruce Coleman; 70 Beecham Pharmaceuticals UK Division; 71 J. B. Gurdon. Cover: N.H.P.A./John Sparks front; N.H.P.A./Stephen Dalton top back, N.H.P.A./Walker bottom back.

Artwork: Tudor Art Agency (Norman Cumming, Ron Jobson, Bernard Robinson, Mike Saunders, David Wright); Dave Etchell and John Ridyard; Irenè Radó-Vajda. **Cover design:** John Strange.

Grove snail
Potter wasp
Acorn worm
Purple heart urchin
Sea squirt
Hemichordates
Echinoderms
Molluscs
Insects
Lancelet
Urochordates
Cephalochordates
Hagfish
Jawless fishes
Asterocerus
Mako shark
Cartilaginous fishes
Stenody
Australian salmon
Bony fishes
Salamander
Amphibians
Placoderms
Box tortoise
Pterichthyodes
Reptiles
Hemicyclaspis
Mallard duck
Birds
Archaeopteryx
Megalosaurus
Pleuracanthus
Macaque monkey
Erythotosuchus
Eusthenopteron (Rhipidistian fish)
Mammals
Maerosystella
Eohippus (early horse)

QUATERNARY
2
Million years ago
TERTIARY
65
CRETACEOUS
135
JURASSIC
193
TRIASSIC
225
PERMIAN
280
CARBONIFEROUS
345
DEVONIAN
395
SILURIAN
435
ORDOVICIAN
500
CAMBRIAN
600
PRECAMBRIAN